MOVIE SONGS FOR ACCORDION

Arranged by Pete Deneff

ISBN 978-1-70515-114-3

Visit Hal Leonard Online at
www.halleonard.com

Contact Us:
Hal Leonard
7777 West Bluemound Road
Milwaukee, WI 53213
Email: info@halleonard.com

In Europe, contact:
Hal Leonard Europe Limited
42 Wigmore Street
Marylebone, London, W1U 2RN
Email: info@halleonardeurope.com

In Australia, contact:
Hal Leonard Australia Pty. Ltd.
4 Lentara Court
Cheltenham, Victoria, 3192 Australia
Email: info@halleonard.com.au

AS TIME GOES BY

from CASABLANCA

Words and Music by
HERMAN HUPFELD

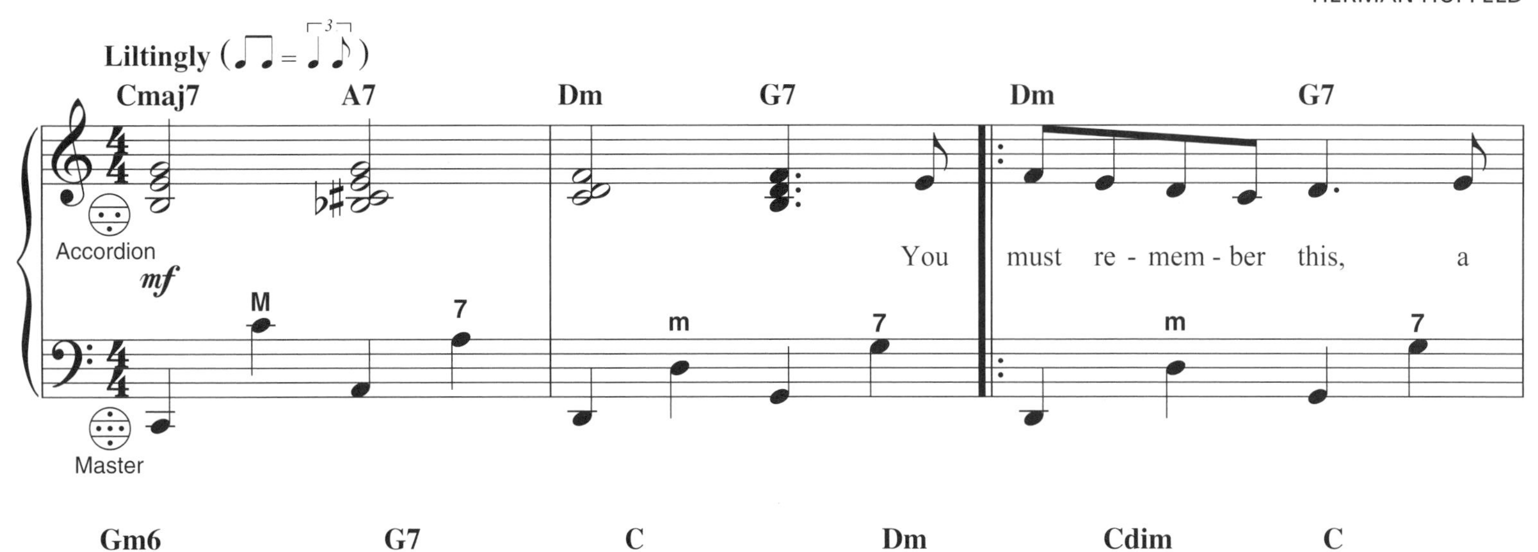

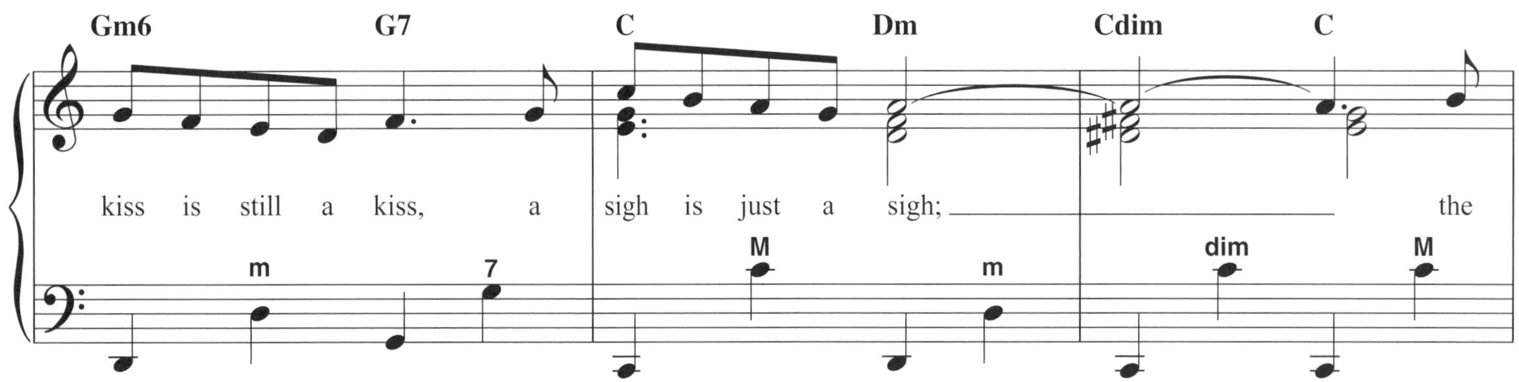

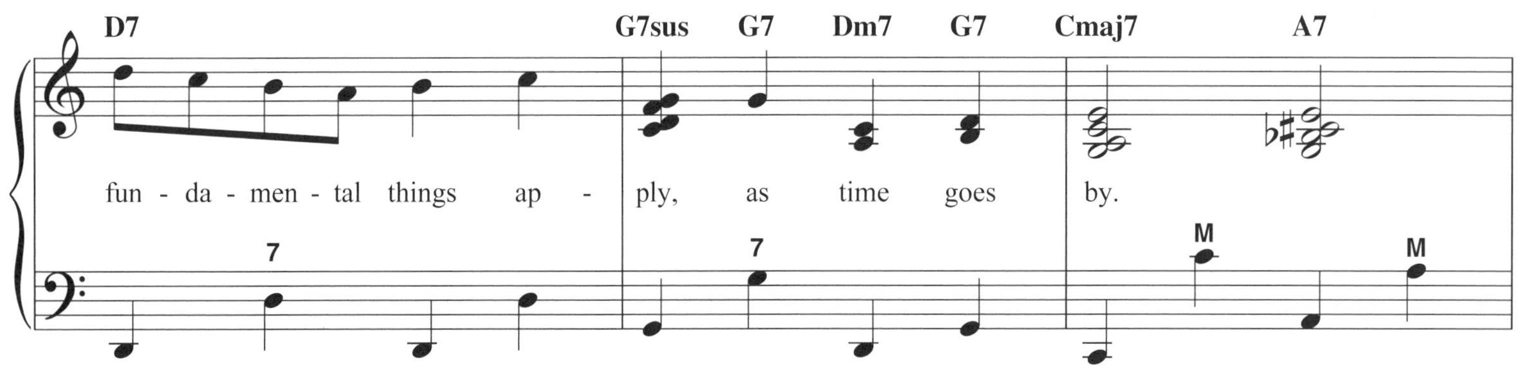

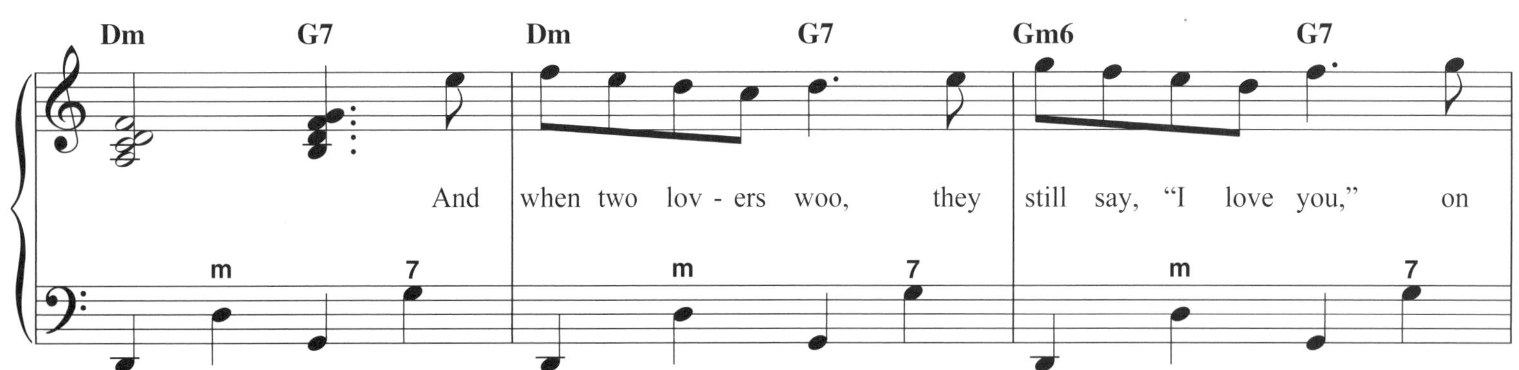

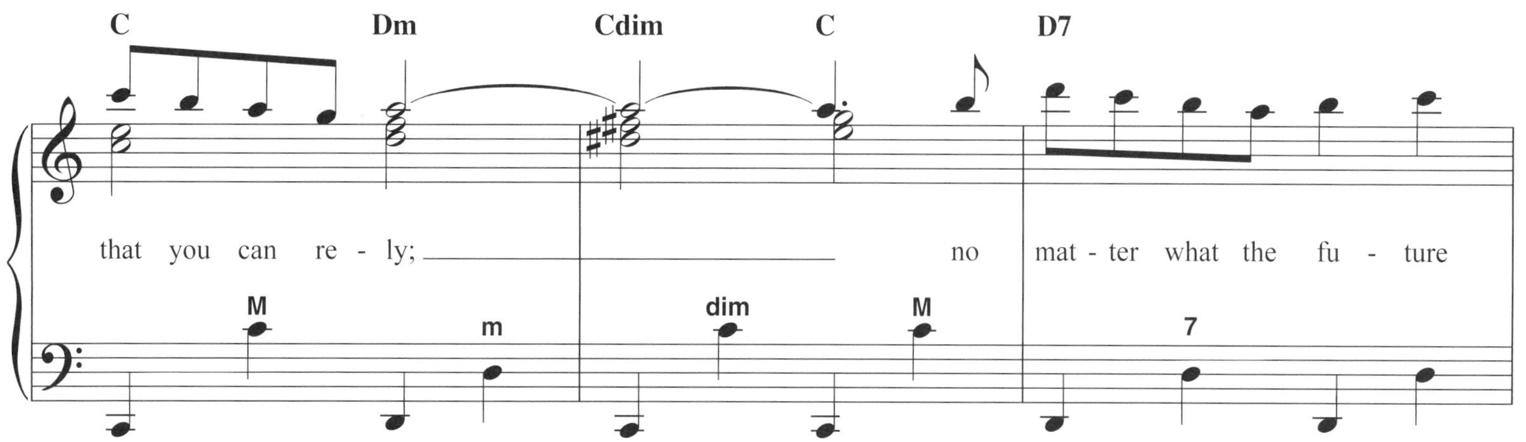
C
Dm
Cdim
C
D7
that you can re - ly;
no
mat - ter what the fu - ture
M
m
dim
M
7

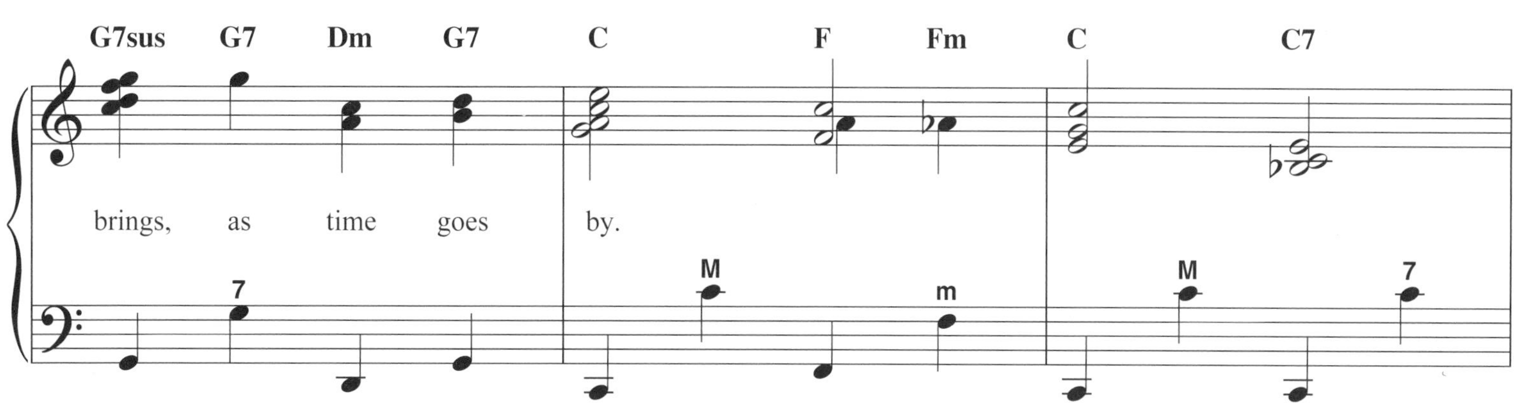
G7sus
G7
Dm
G7
C
F
Fm
C
C7
brings, as time goes by.
7
M
m
M
7

F
A7
Dm
Moon-light and love songs
nev - er out of date,
hearts full of pas - sion,
M
7
m

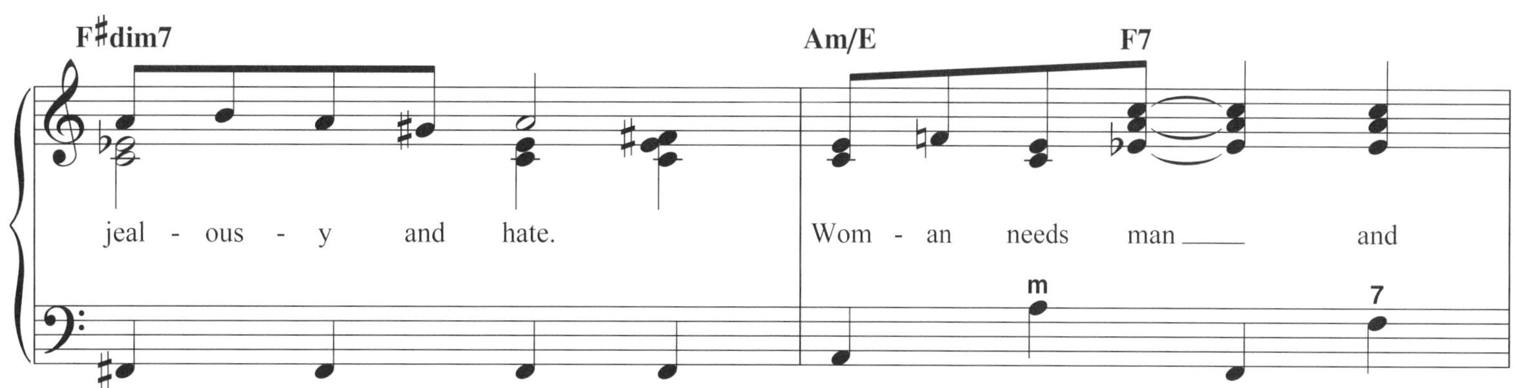
F♯dim7
Am/E
F7
jeal - ous - y and hate.
Wom - an needs man and
m
7

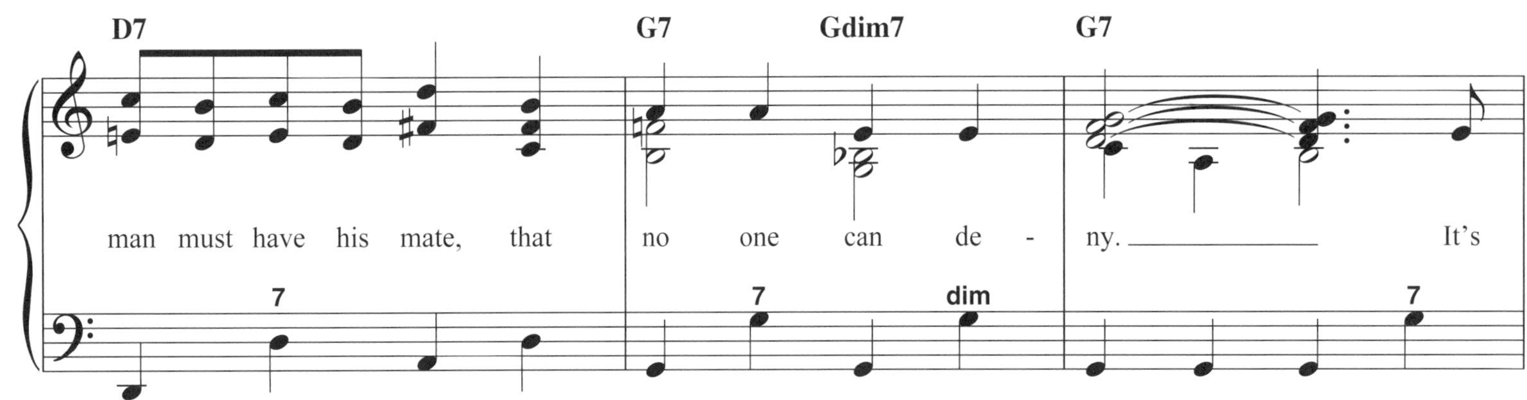
D7
G7
Gdim7
G7
man must have his mate, that no one can de - ny. It's
7
7
dim
7

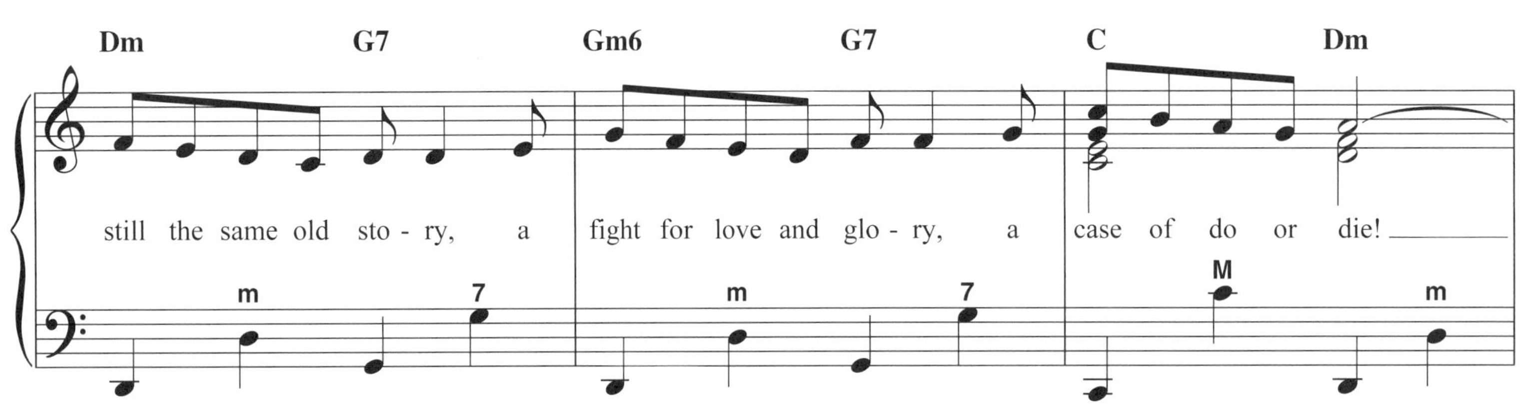
Dm
G7
Gm6
G7
C
Dm
still the same old sto - ry, a fight for love and glo - ry, a case of do or die!
m
7
m
7
M
m

Cdim
C
D7
C
A7
The world will al - ways wel - come lov - ers, as
dim
M
7
M
7

1.
2.
Dm7
G7
C
A7
D7
G7
C
B♭7
C
time goes by. You by.
m
7
M

CHARIOTS OF FIRE

from the Feature Film CHARIOTS OF FIRE

By VANGELIS

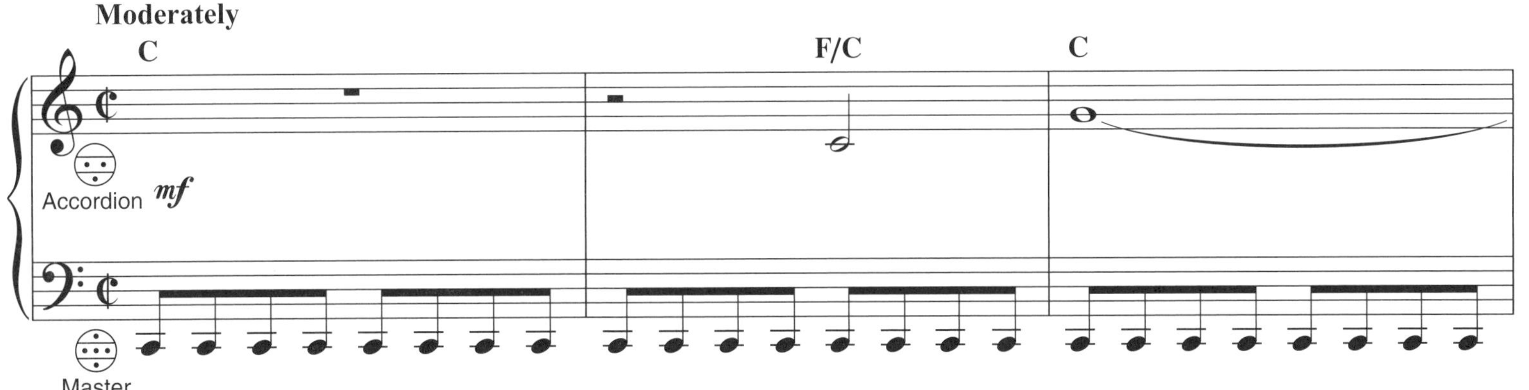

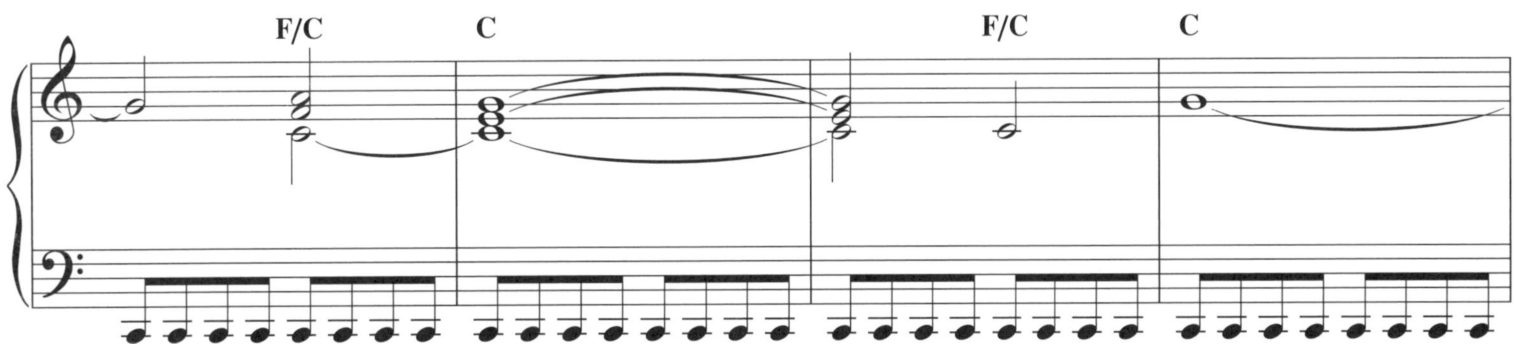

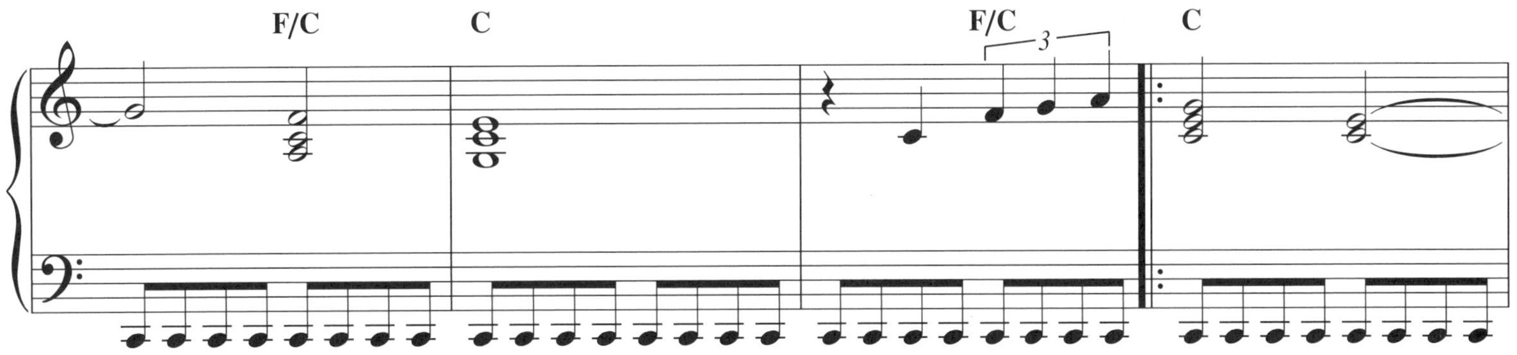

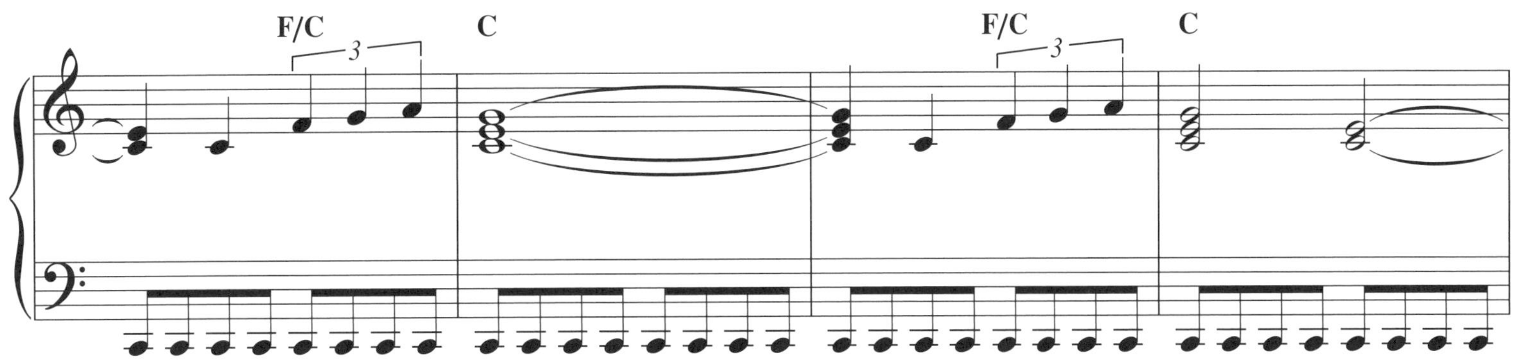

F/C
C
1.
F/C
2.
f
Em
F
C
Em
G7
C
Em
F
C
G
1.
C
2.
C
F/C
mf
C
F/C
C
F/C
C
F/C

C
1.
F/C
2.
Em
F
f
C
Em
G7
C
Em
F
C
G
1.
C
2.
C
F/C
C
F/C
C
mf
mp
F/C
C
p
M

DAYS OF WINE AND ROSES

from DAYS OF WINE AND ROSES

Lyrics by JOHNNY MERCER
Music by HENRY MANCINI

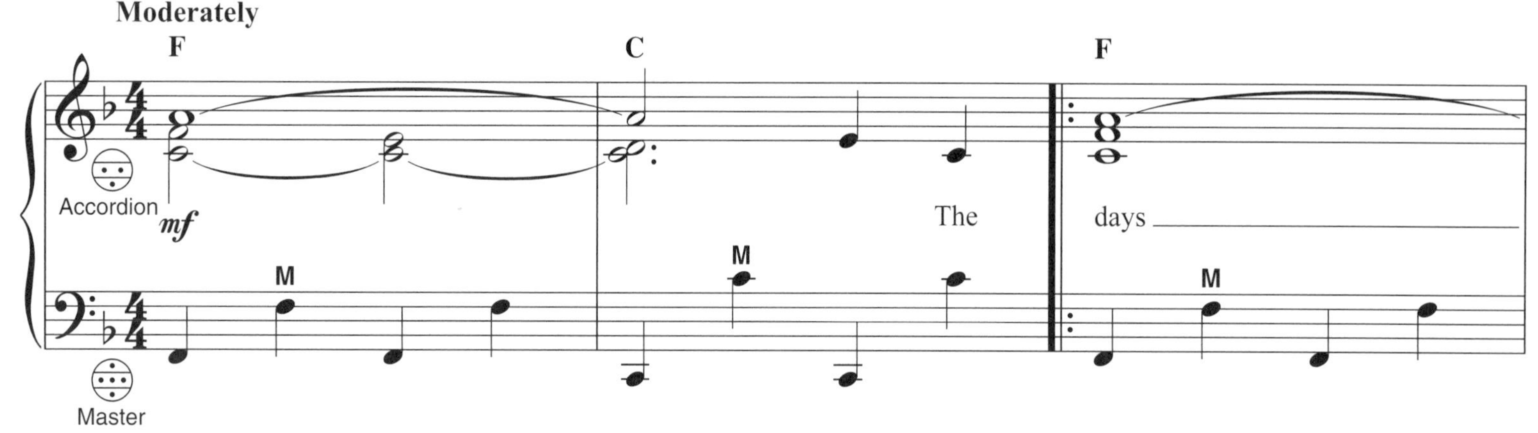

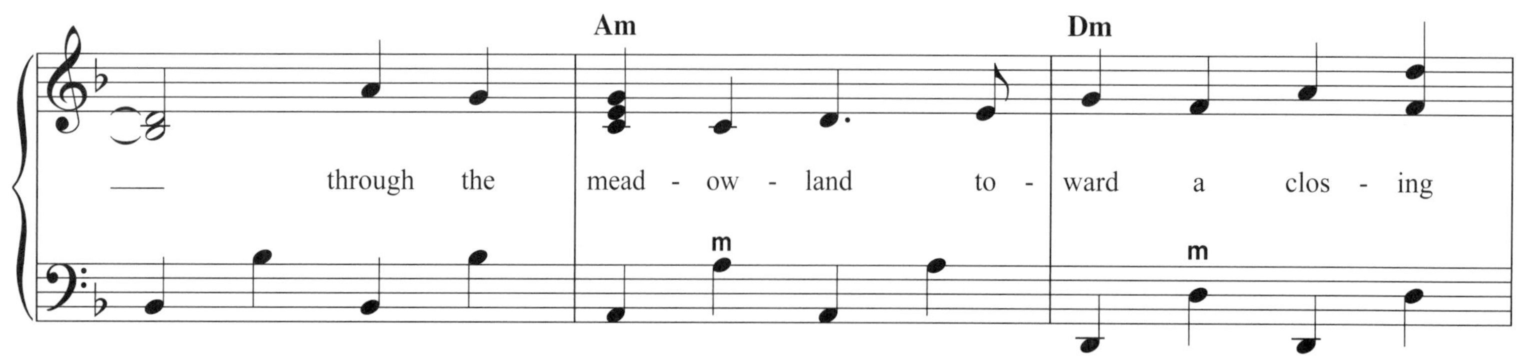

Gm
Em7♭5
A9
door, a door marked "Nev - er - more," that
m
dim
7

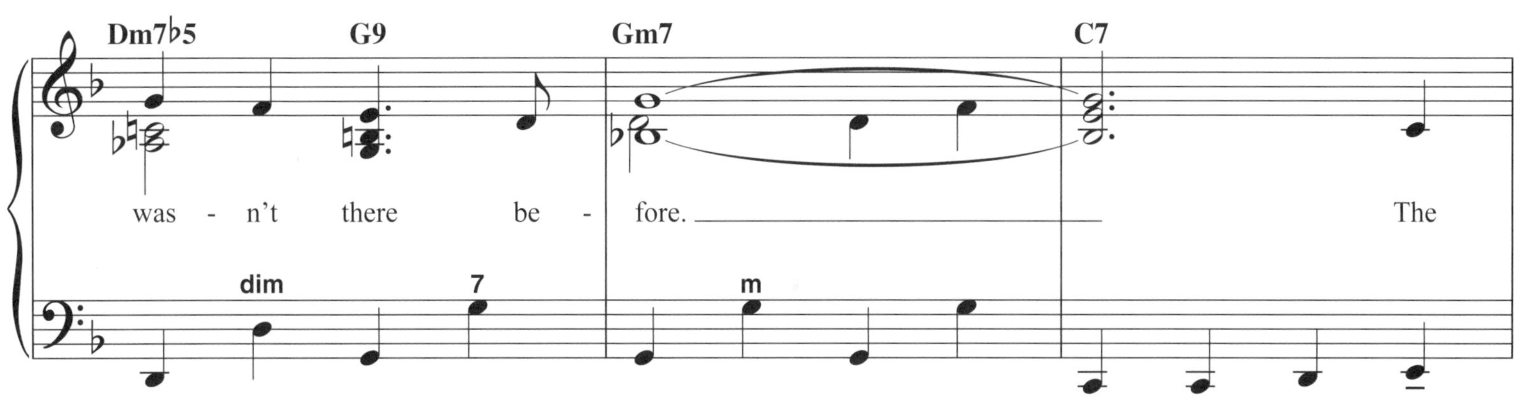
Dm7♭5
G9
Gm7
C7
was - n't there be - fore. The
dim
7
m

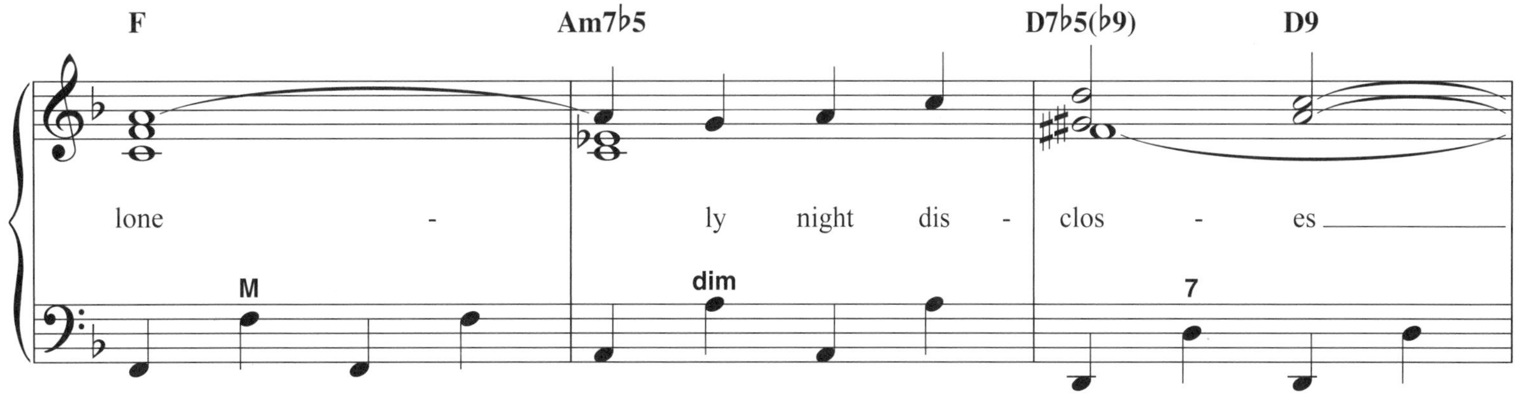
F
Am7♭5
D7♭5(♭9)
D9
lone - ly night dis - clos - es
M
dim
7

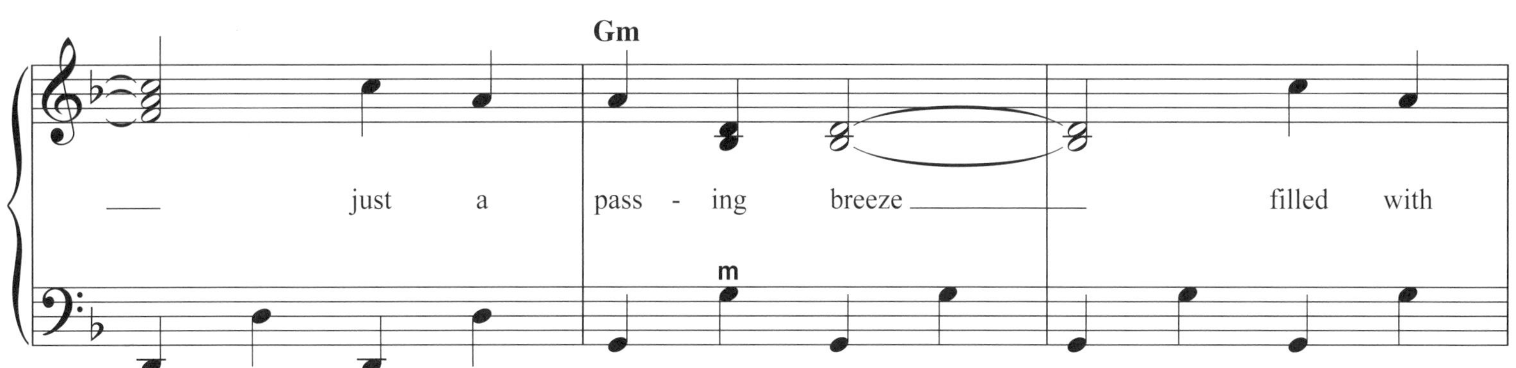
Gm
just a pass - ing breeze filled with
m

B♭m
Am
mem - o - ries of the gold - en smile that
m
m

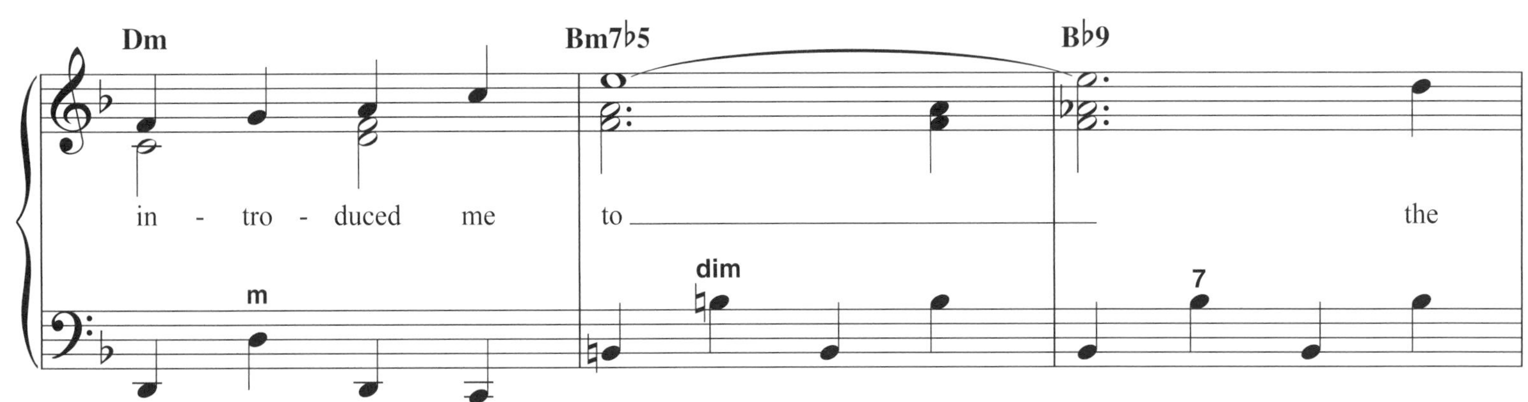
Dm
Bm7♭5
B♭9
in - tro - duced me to the
m
dim
7

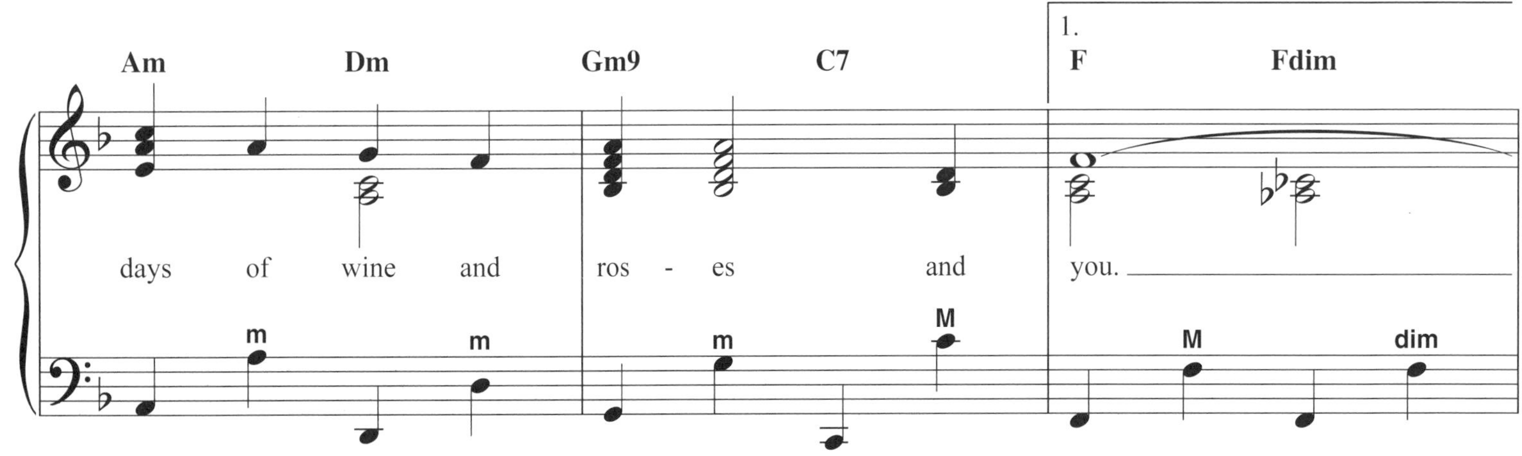
1.
Am
Dm
Gm9
C7
F
Fdim
days of wine and ros - es and you.
m
m
m
M
M
dim

2.
Gm7
C7
F
B♭m
F6
The
you.
rall.
m
M
M
m
M

HOW FAR I'LL GO

from MOANA

Music and Lyrics by
LIN-MANUEL MIRANDA

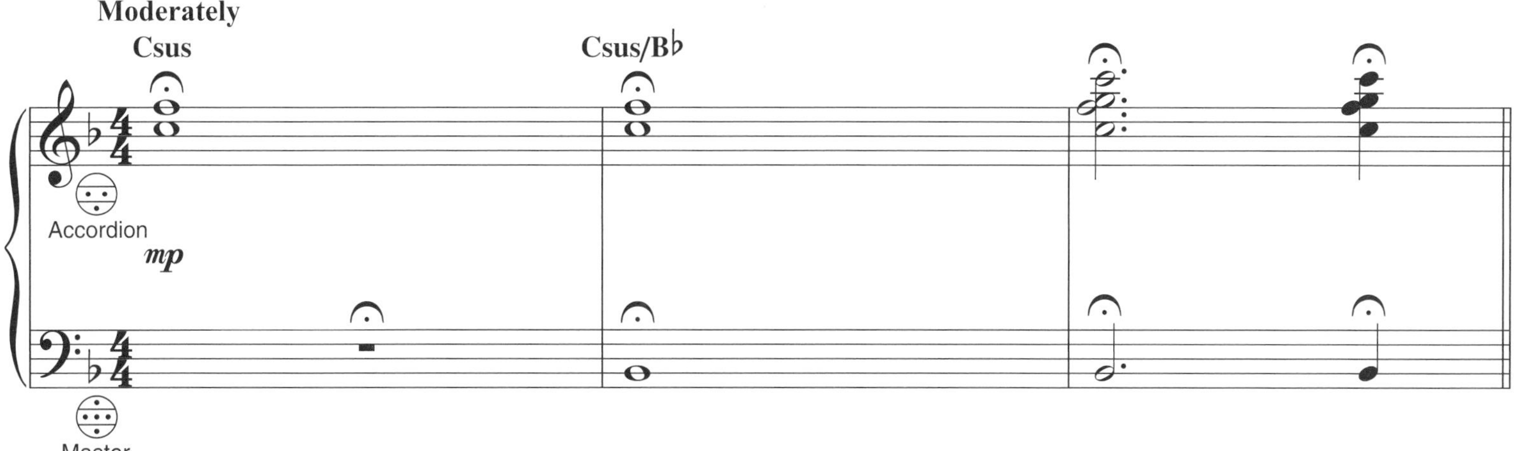

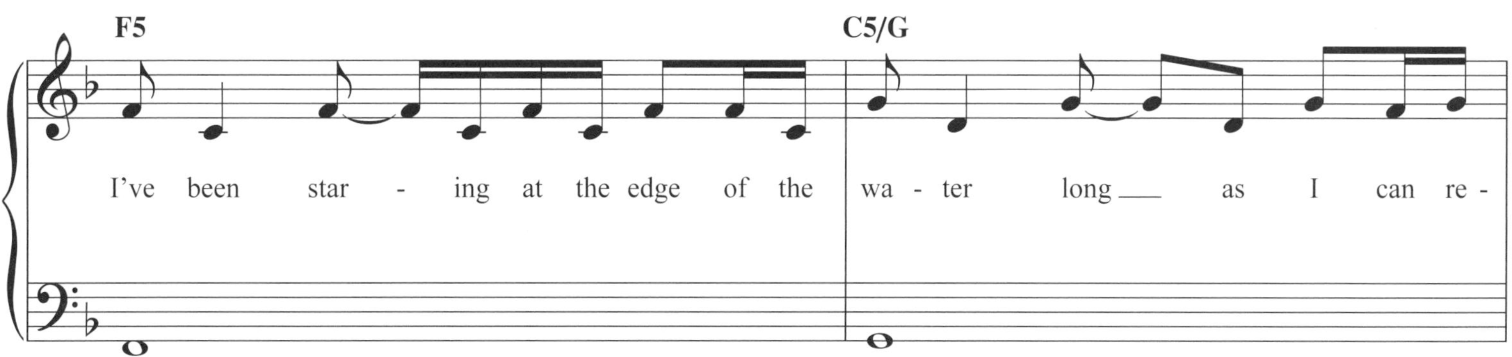

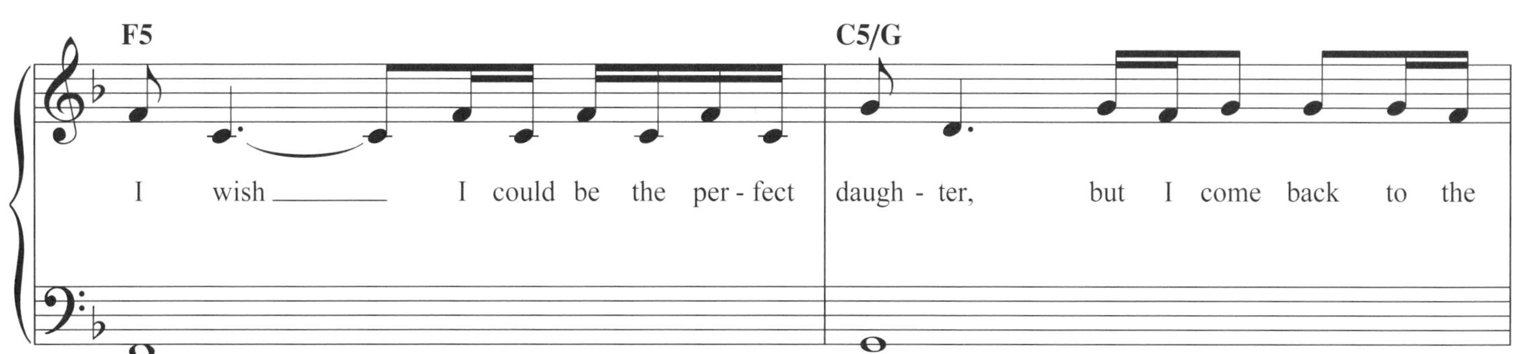

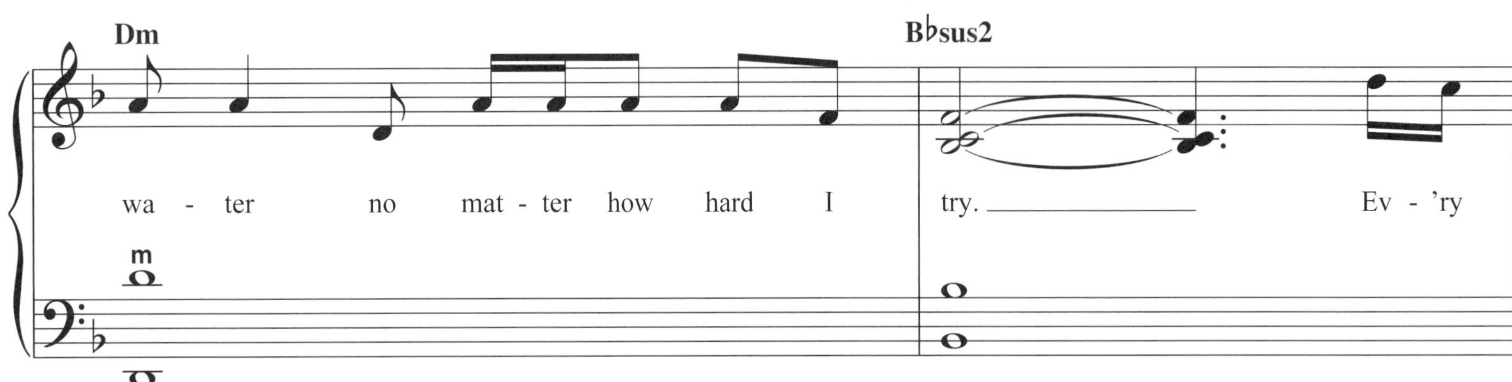
Dm
Bbsus2
wa - ter no mat - ter how hard I
try. ______
Ev - 'ry
m
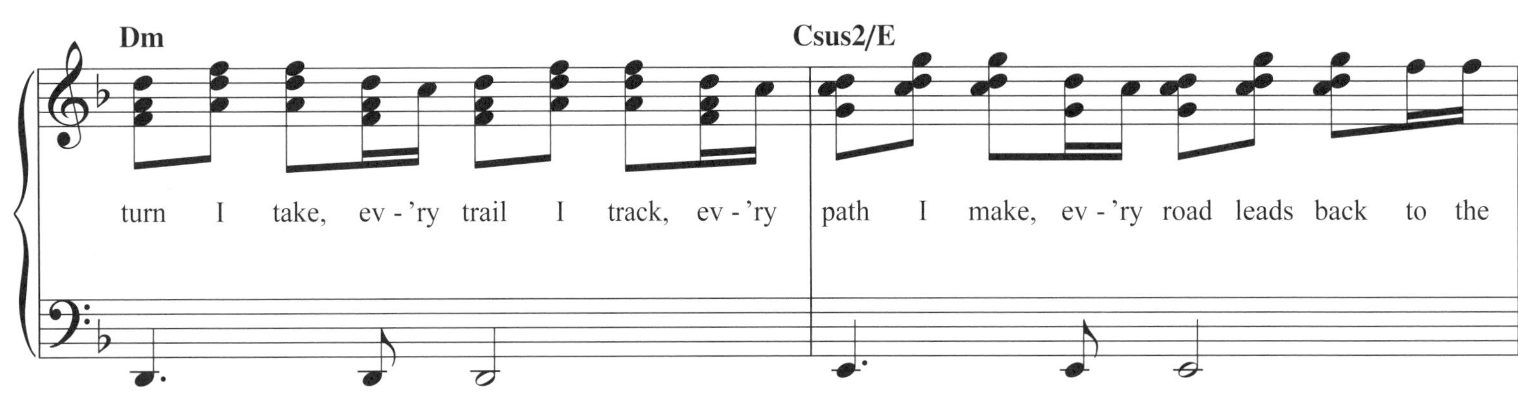
Dm
Csus2/E
turn I take, ev - 'ry trail I track, ev - 'ry
path I make, ev - 'ry road leads back to the
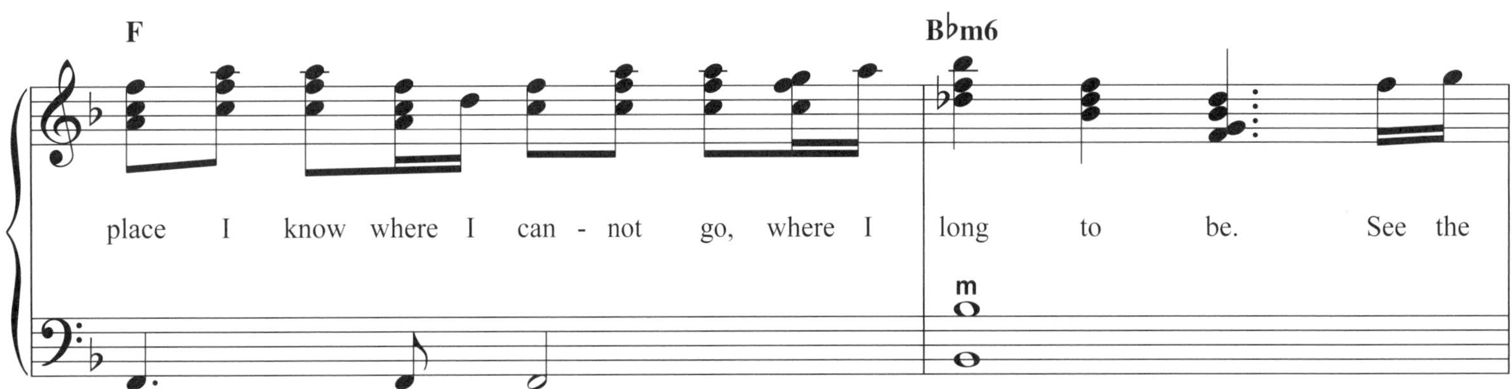
F
Bbm6
place I know where I can - not go, where I
long to be. See the
m

F5
Csus
C
line where the sky meets the sea, it calls ___
me, ______ and no one
M
M

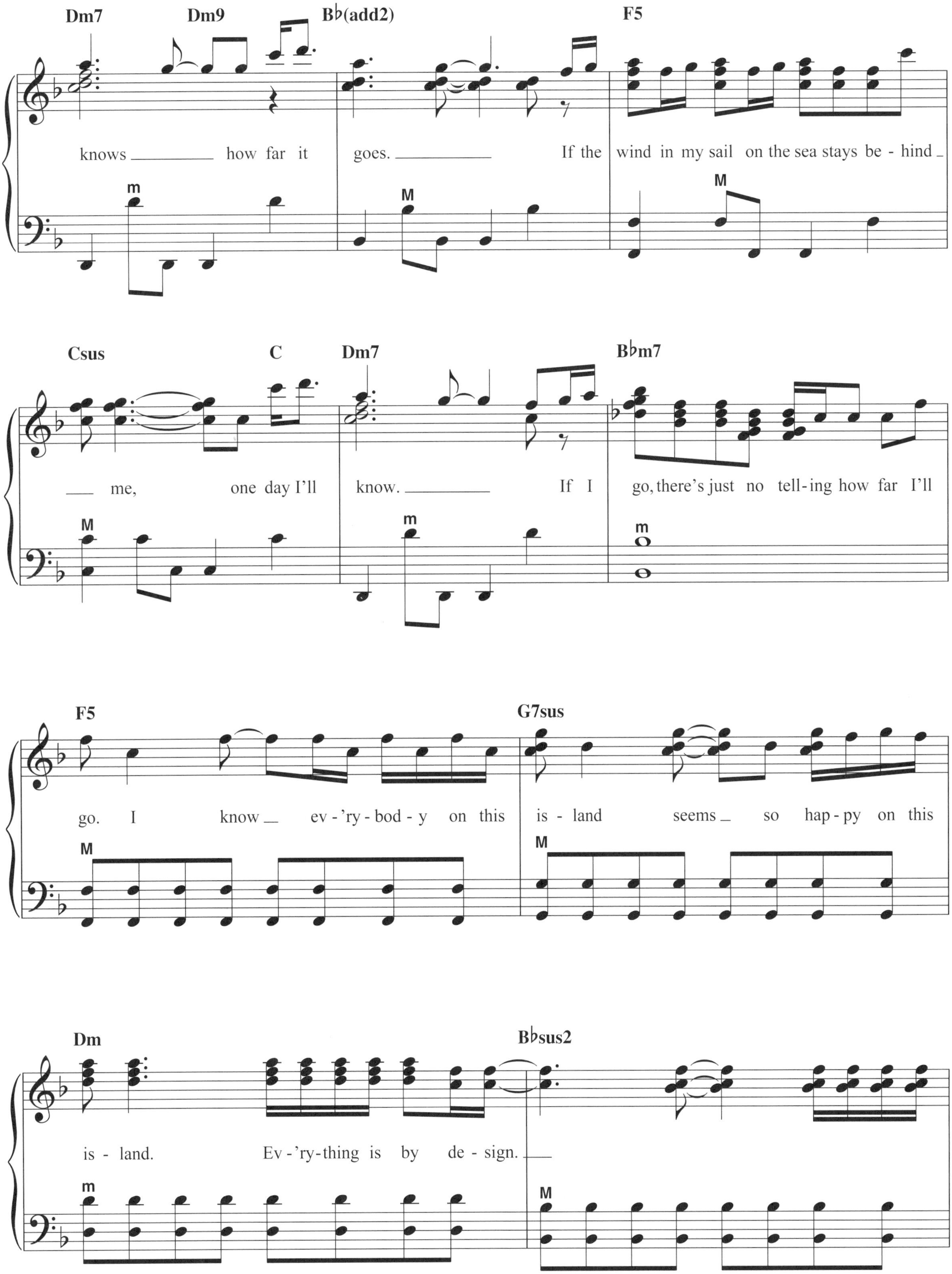

Dm7
Dm9
B♭(add2)
F5
knows ___ how far it goes. ___ If the wind in my sail on the sea stays be - hind
m
M
M
Csus
C
Dm7
B♭m7
___ me, one day I'll know. ___ If I go, there's just no tell-ing how far I'll
M
m
m
F5
G7sus
go. I know ___ ev - 'ry - bod - y on this is - land seems ___ so hap - py on this
M
M
Dm
B♭sus2
is - land. Ev - 'ry-thing is by de - sign. ___
m
M

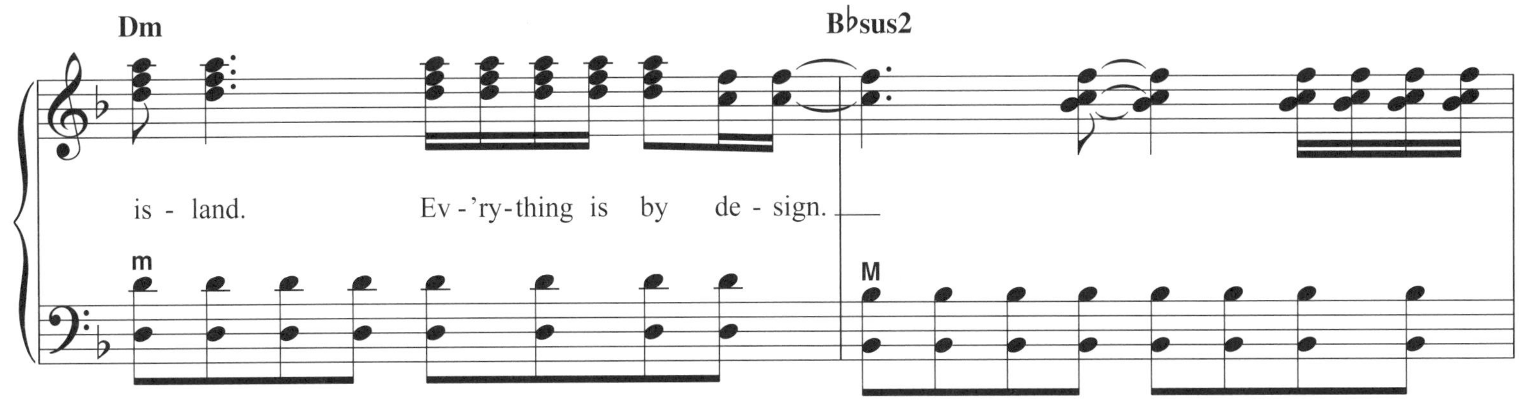

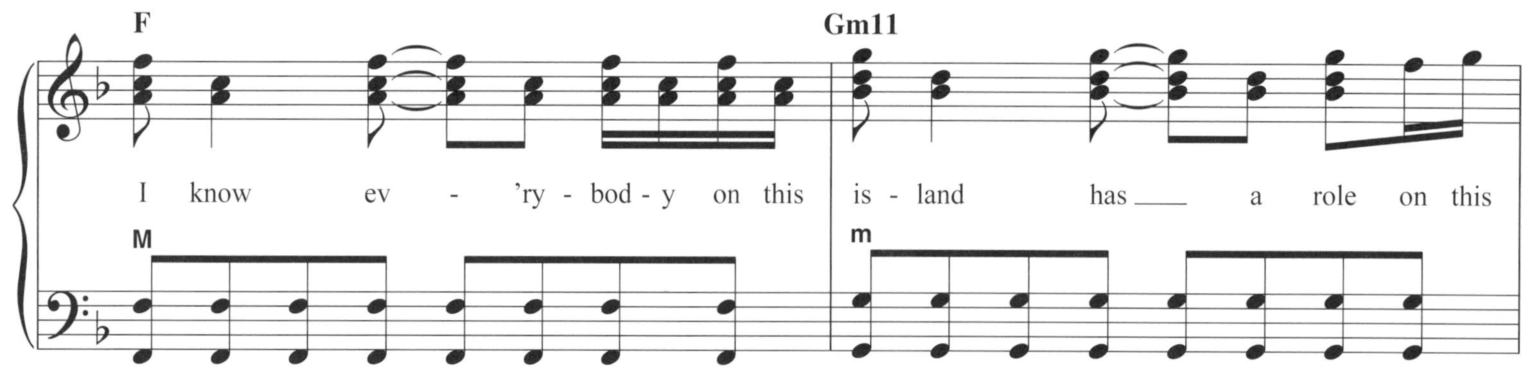
F
Gm11
I know ev - 'ry - bod - y on this is - land has a role on this
M
m

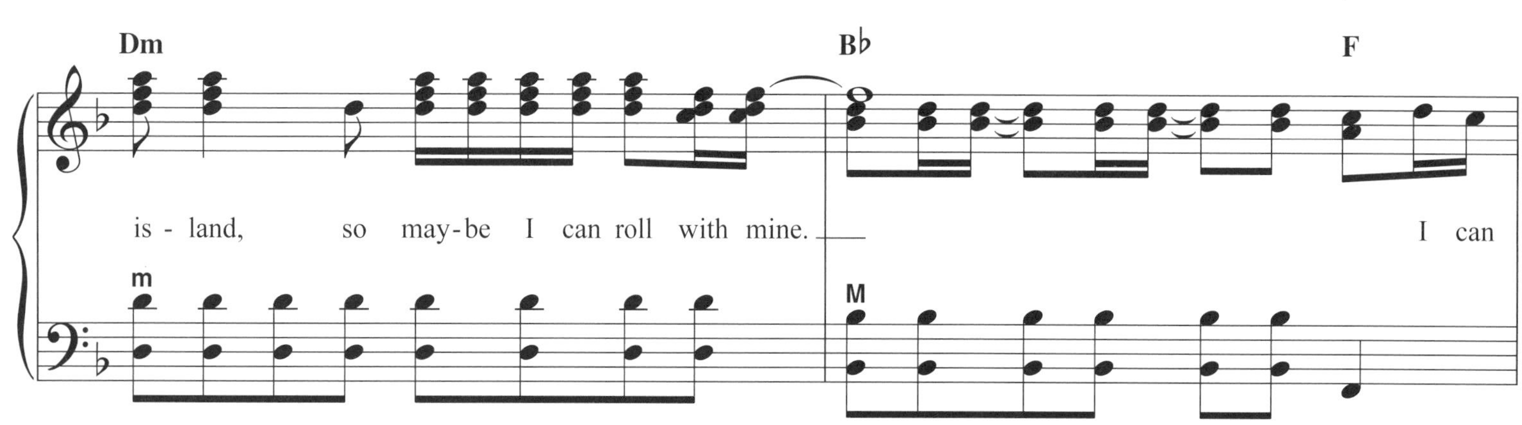
Dm
B♭
F
is - land, so may-be I can roll with mine. I can
m
M

Dm
Csus2/E
lead with pride, I can make us strong. I'll be sat - is - fied if I play a - long, but the

F
B♭m
voice in - side sings a dif - f'rent song. What is wrong with me?
m

B♭m6
F
See the light as it shines on the sea: it's blind -
m
M

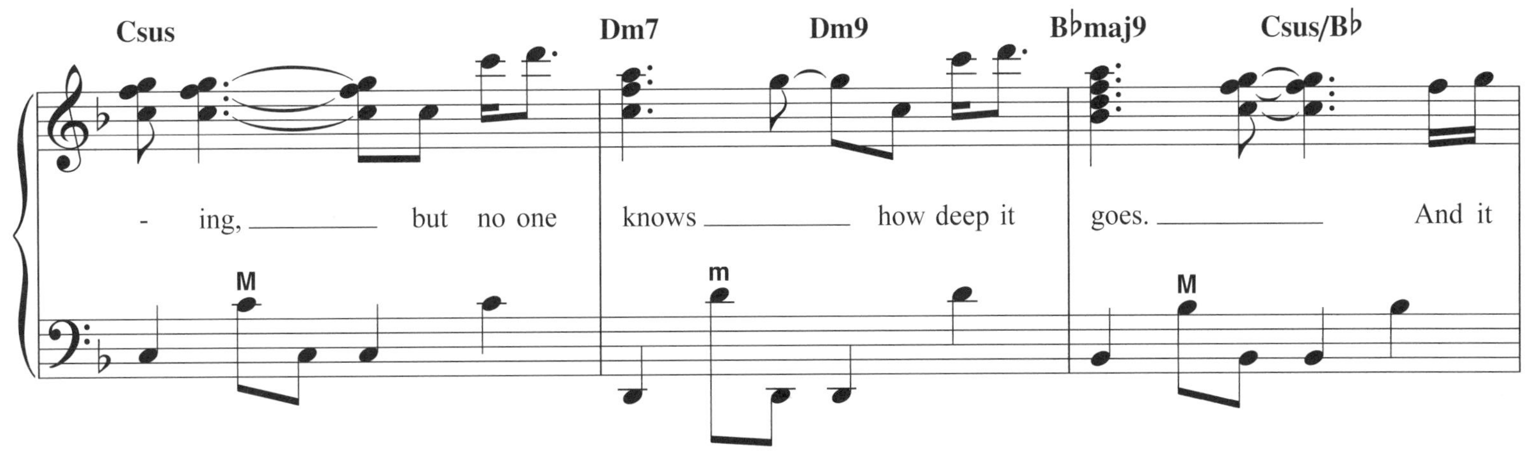
Csus
Dm7
Dm9
B♭maj9
Csus/B♭
- ing, but no one
knows how deep it
goes. And it
M
m
M

F
Csus
C
seems like it's call - ing out to me, so come find
me and let me
M
M

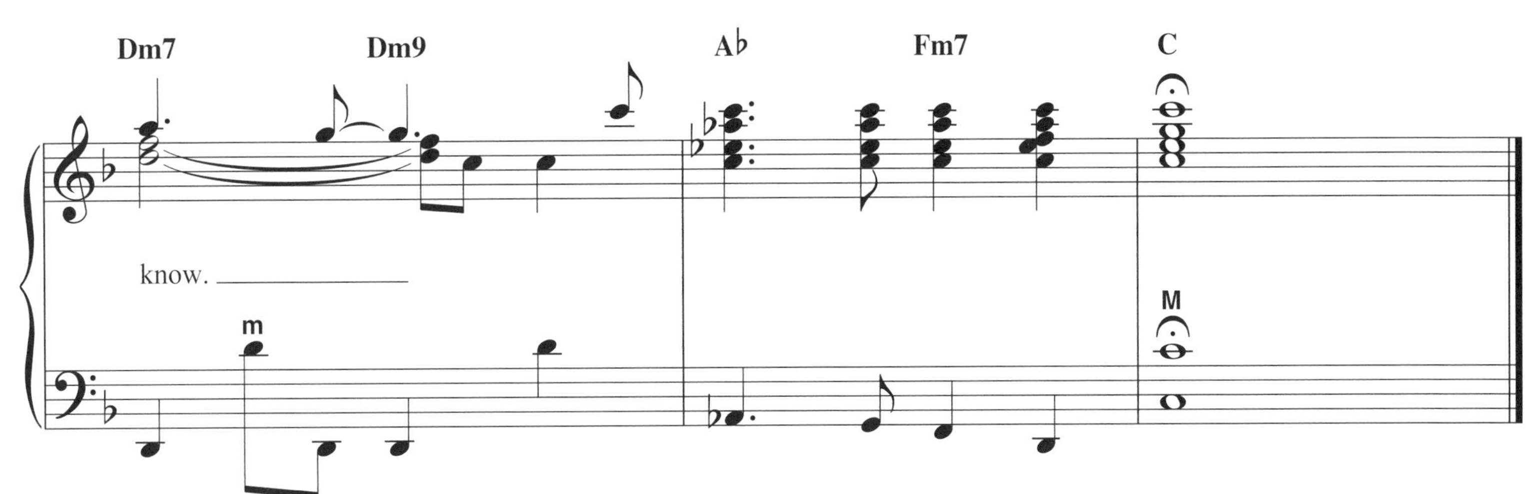
Dm7
Dm9
A♭
Fm7
C
know.
m
M

FOOTLOOSE

Theme from the Paramount Motion Picture FOOTLOOSE

Words by DEAN PITCHFORD
Music by KENNY LOGGINS

D/A
A
for what?
in your heart
Oh, tell me
you're burn - in',
what I got.
yearn - in' for some,

D
I've got this
some - bod - y to
feel - in'
tell you
that time's just
that life ain't

hold - in' me down.
pass - in' you by.
A

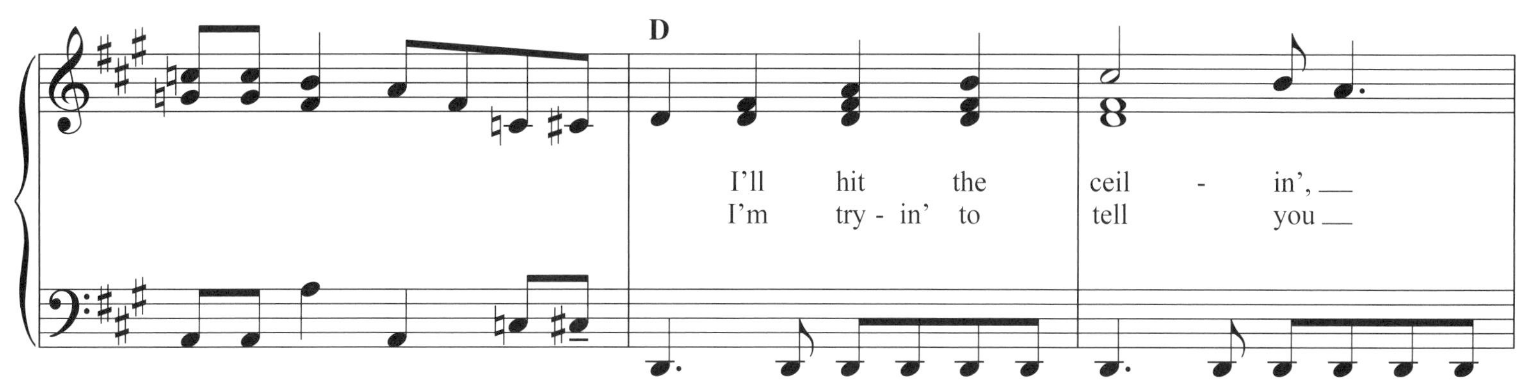
D
I'll hit the
I'm try - in' to
ceil - in',
tell you

D♯dim
B7
E
F♯m7
or else I'll tear up this town.
it will if you don't e - ven try.

Gdim7
E/G♯
A
D/A
You can fly if you'd on - ly cut loose, foot -
To-night I got - ta cut loose, foot -
M

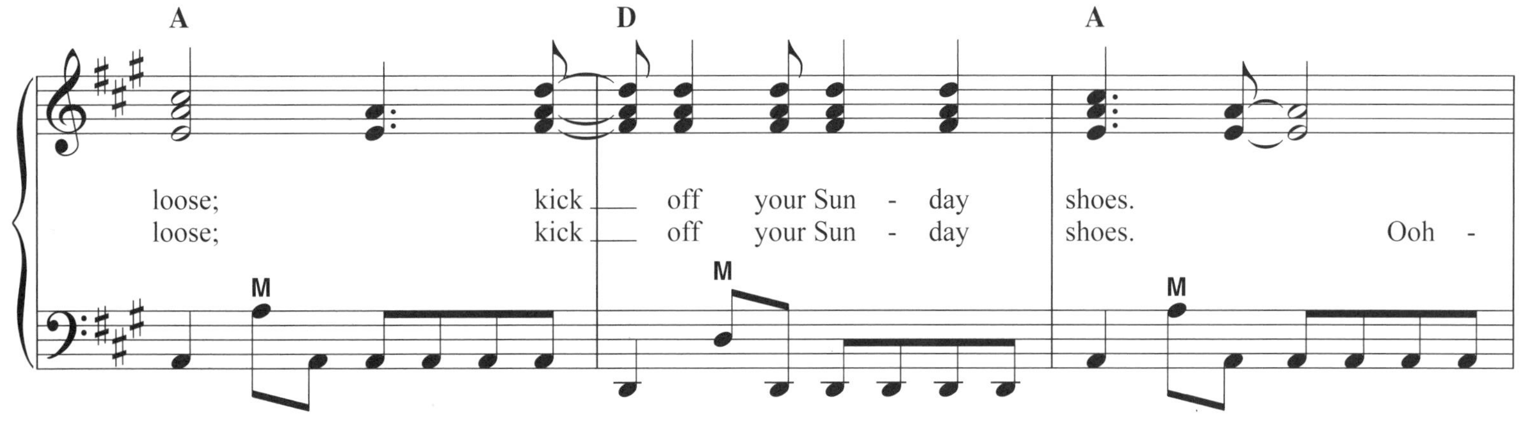
A
D
A
loose; kick off your Sun - day shoes.
loose; kick off your Sun - day shoes. Ooh -
M
M
M

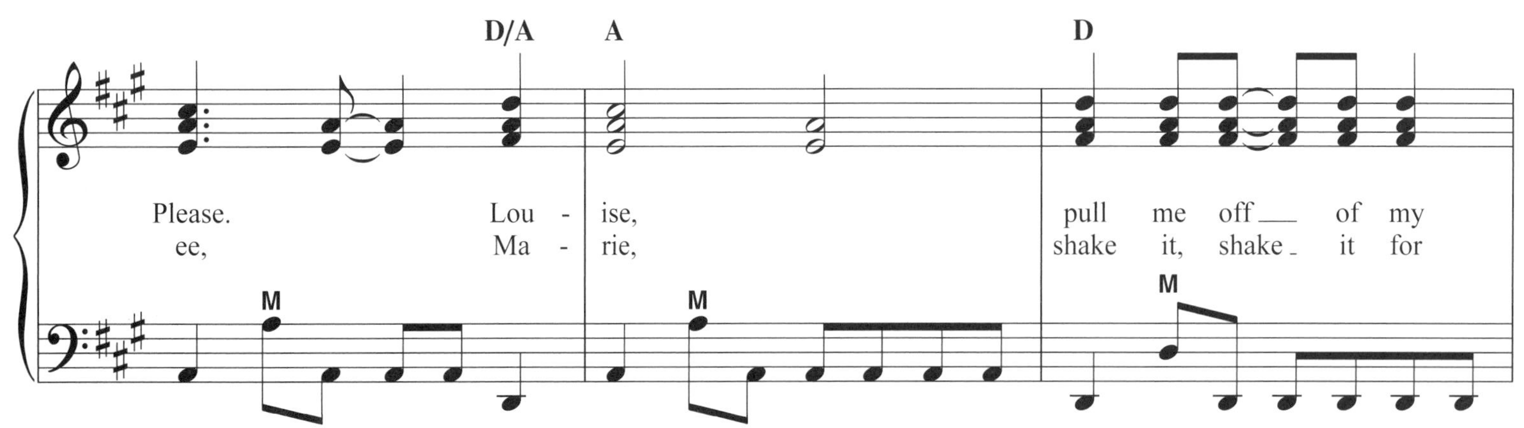
D/A
A
D
Please. Lou - ise, pull me off of my
ee, Ma - rie, shake it, shake it for
M
M
M

A
D/A
A
knees.
me.
Jack,
Whoa,
get
Mi -
back;
lo,
come
come
M
D
A
D/A
on
on,
be - fore
come on
we
let's
crack.
go.
Lose
Lose
your
your
G
blues,
blues,
ev - 'ry - bod - y
cut
foot -
loose.

HOW DOES A MOMENT LAST FOREVER

from BEAUTY AND THE BEAST

Music by ALAN MENKEN
Lyrics by TIM RICE

Bb Gm7 Cm7 Dm7 Gm7 Am7
still. Love lives on in - side our hearts and al - ways
M m m m m

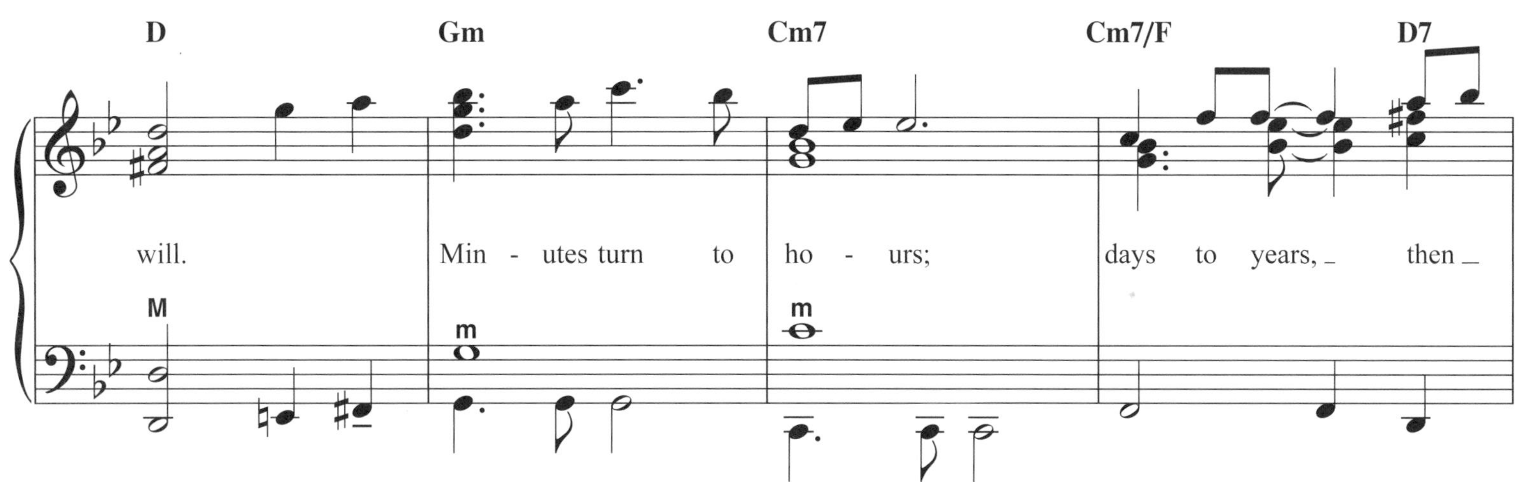
D Gm Cm7 Cm7/F D7
will. Min - utes turn to ho - urs; days to years, then
M m m

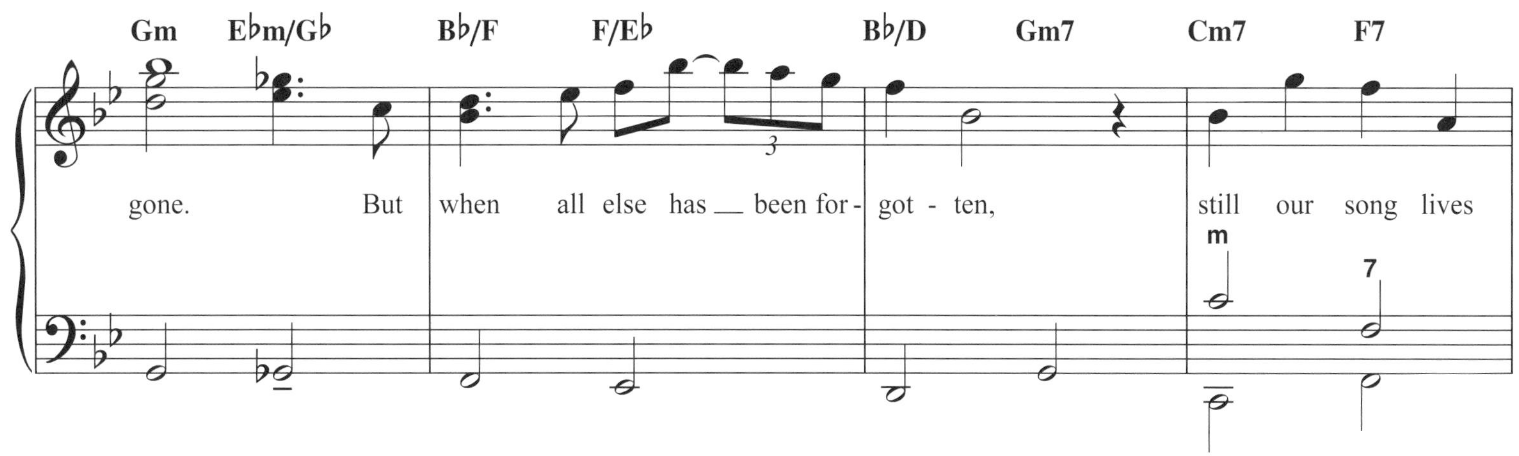
Gm Ebm/Gb Bb/F F/Eb Bb/D Gm7 Cm7 F7
gone. But when all else has been for - got - ten, still our song lives
3
m 7

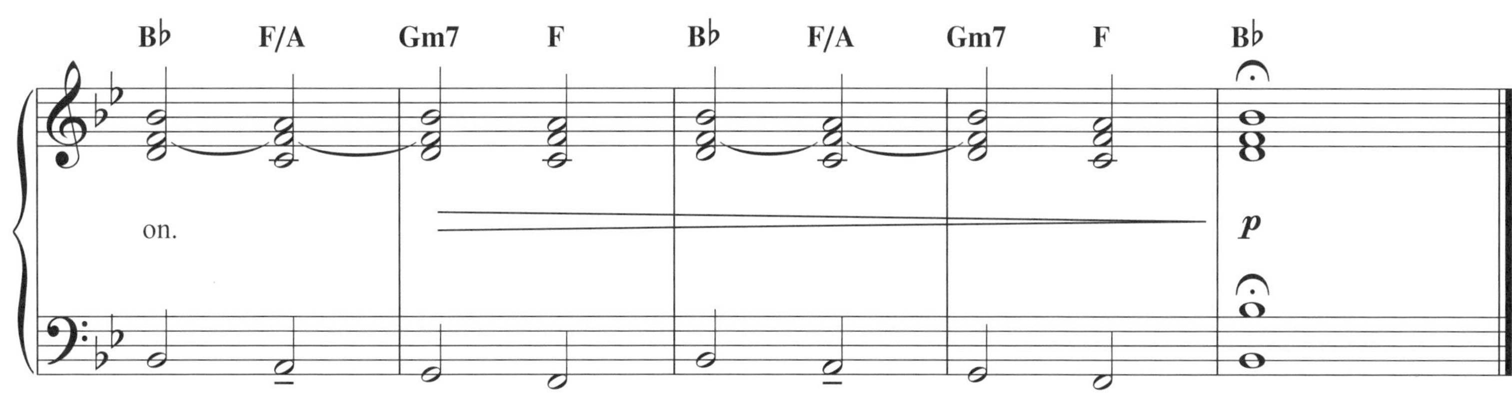
Bb F/A Gm7 F Bb F/A Gm7 F Bb
on.
p

I WILL ALWAYS LOVE YOU

featured in THE BODYGUARD

Words and Music by
DOLLY PARTON

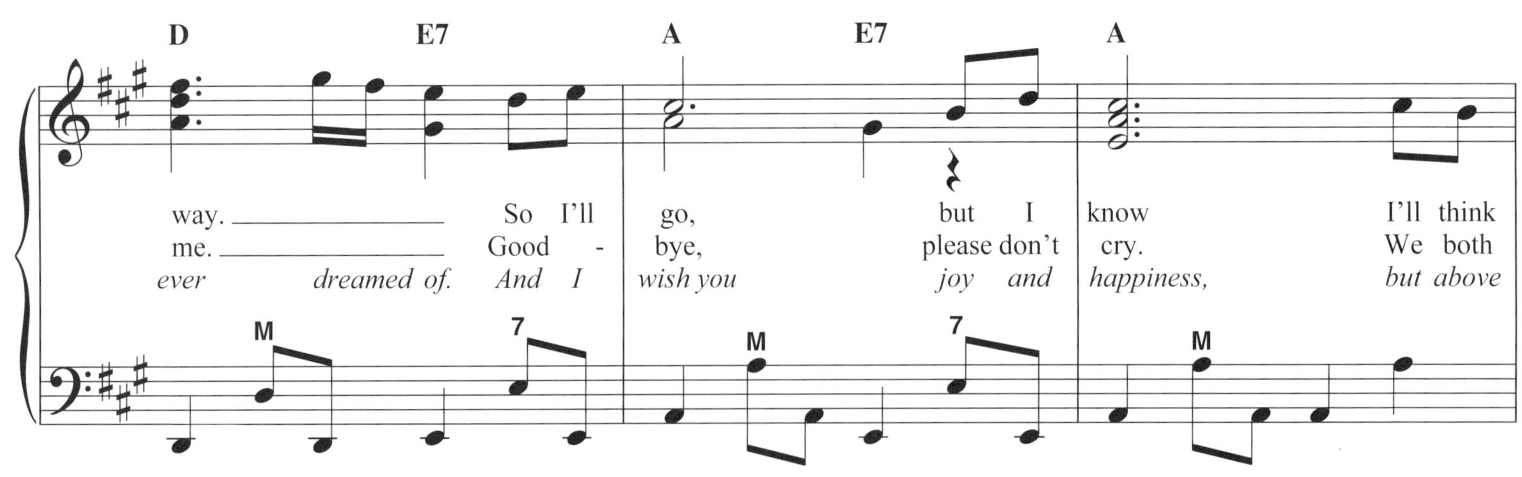

F♯m A/E D E7 A F♯m
of you each step of the way. And
know that I'm not what you need. But
all of this, I wish you love. And
I will
D E7 A F♯m D E7
al - ways love you. I will al - ways love
1., 2.
A D A E7
you.
Bit - ter -
(Spoken): I
3.
A F♯m
you.
D E D E A
I will al - ways love you.

LIVE AND LET DIE

from LIVE AND LET DIE

Words and Music by PAUL McCARTNEY and LINDA McCARTNEY

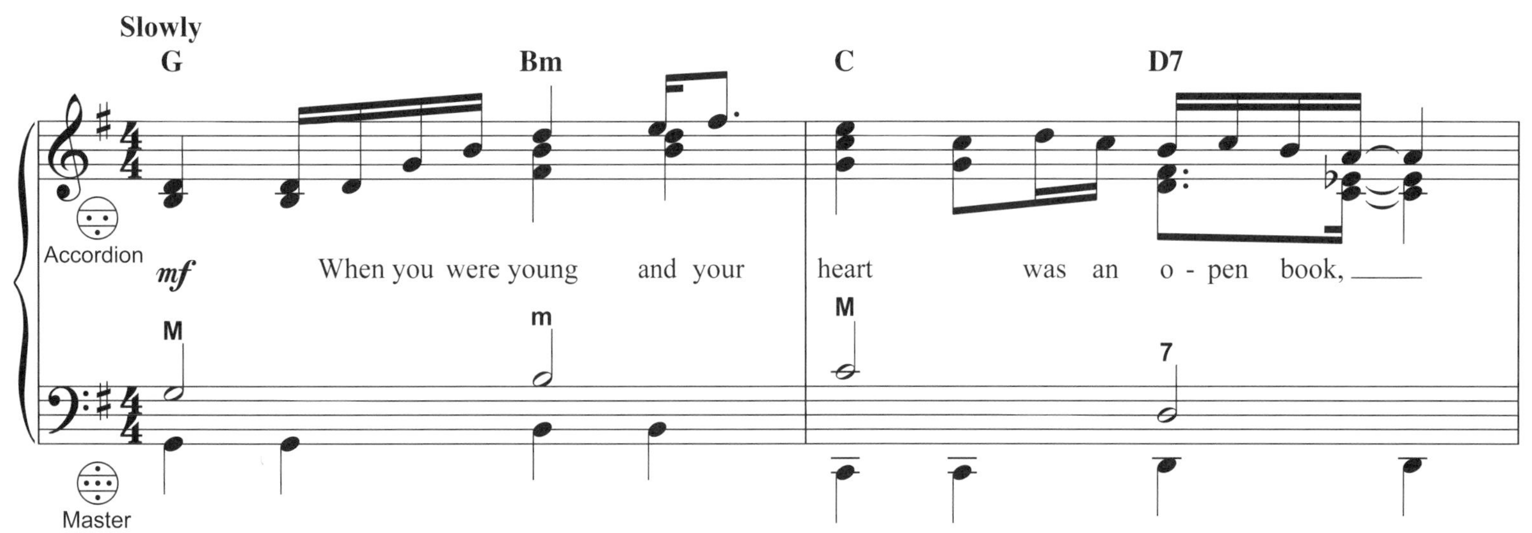

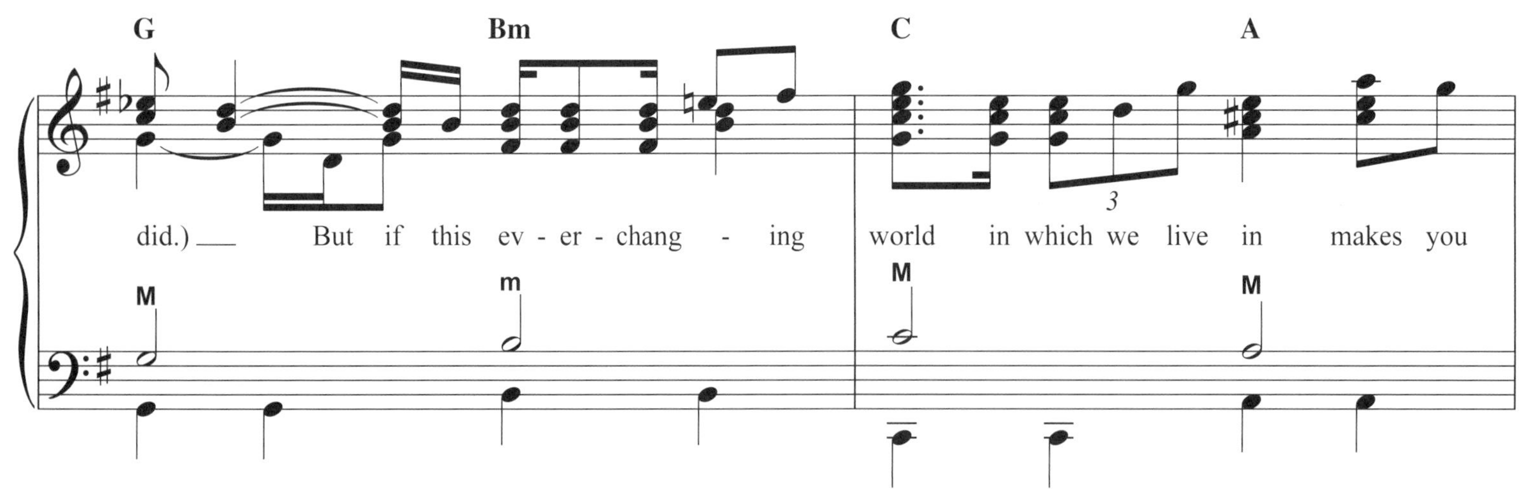

D
Bb
give in and cry,
say live and let die!
M
M

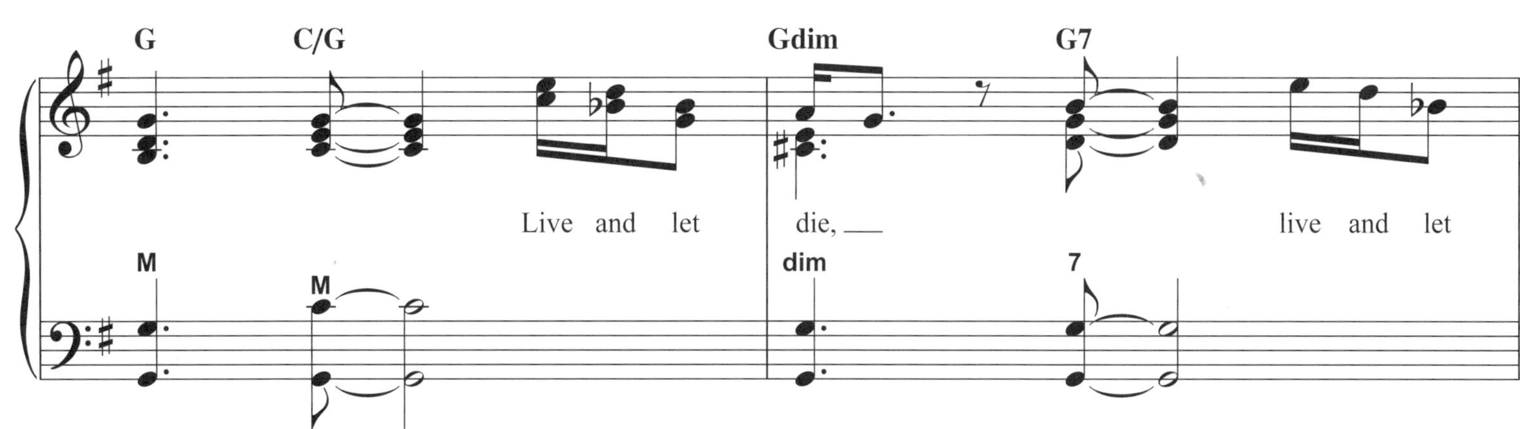
G
C/G
Gdim
G7
Live and let
die,
live and let
M
M
dim
7

C/G
die,
live and let
die.
M

Faster
Gm
ff

To Coda

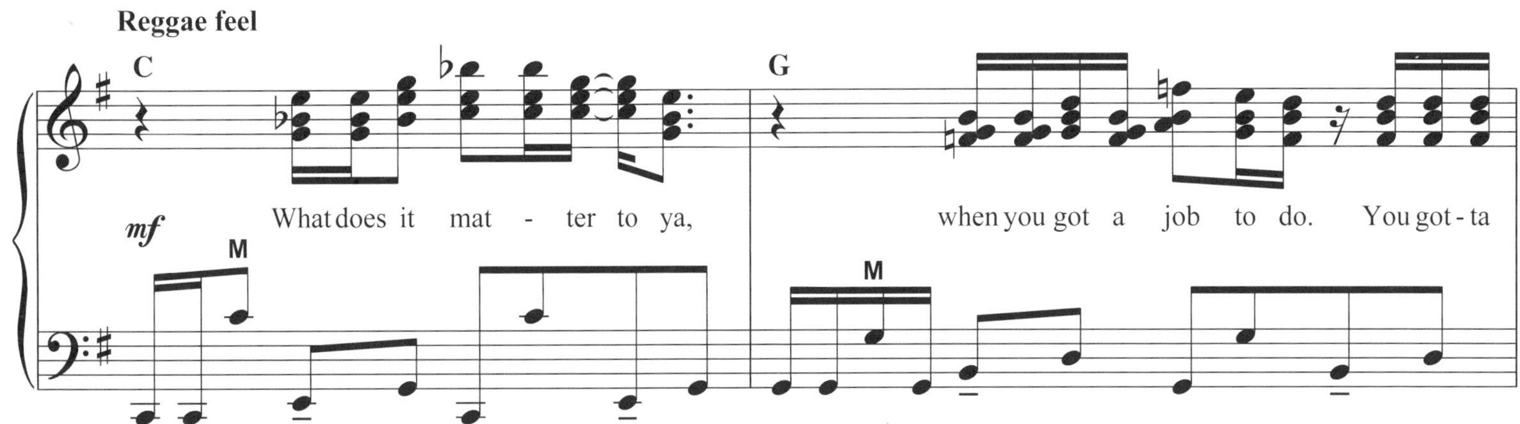
Reggae feel
C
G
mf
What does it mat - ter to ya,
when you got a job to do. You got - ta
M
M

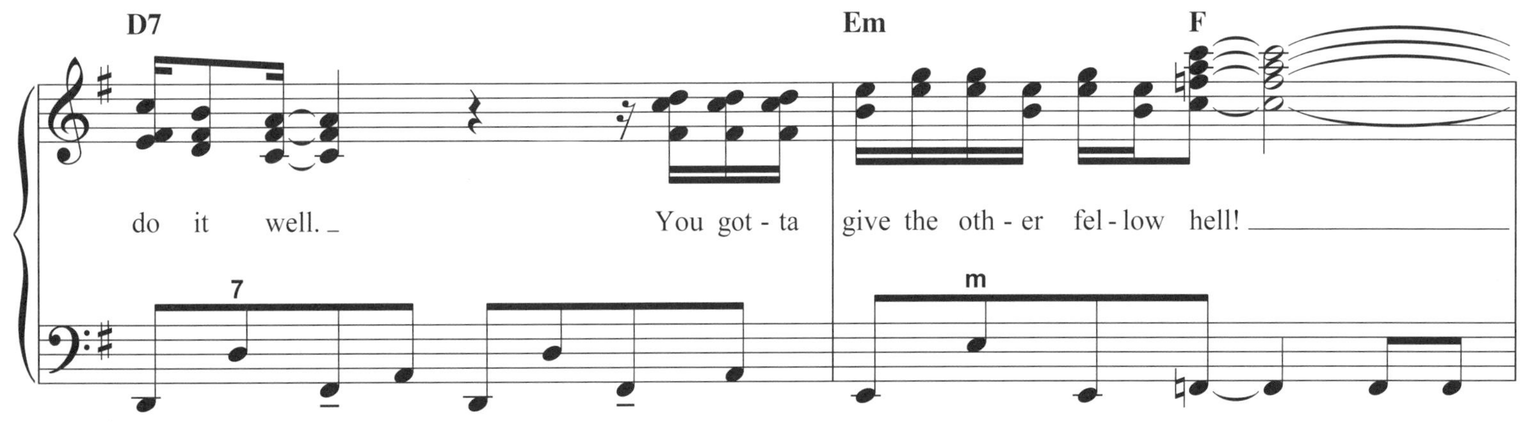
D7
Em
F
do it well.
You got - ta
give the oth - er fel - low hell!
7
m

Faster
Gm
ff
M

D.C. al Coda

CODA

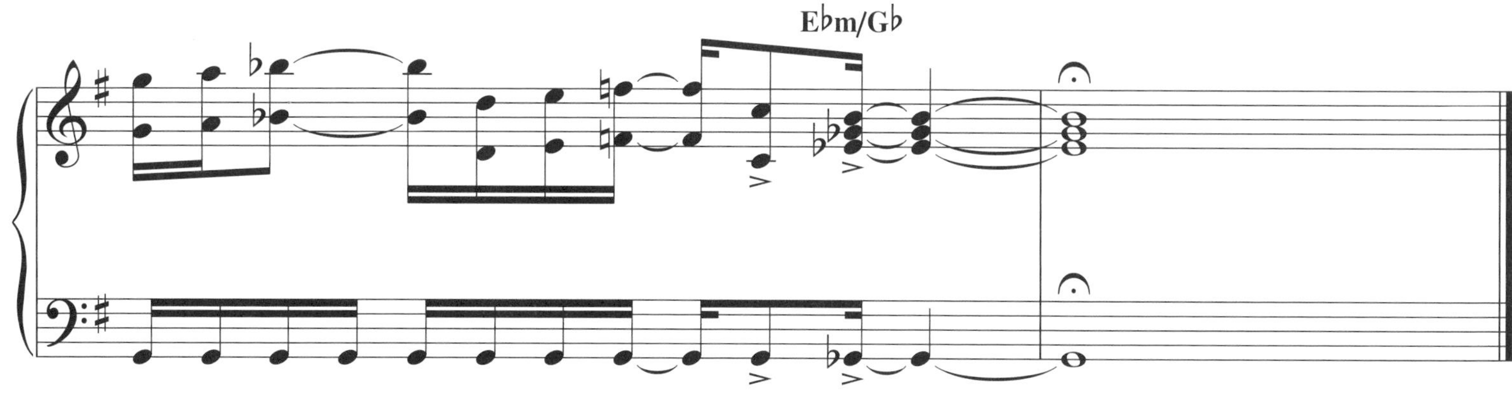
E♭m/G♭

THE LOOK OF LOVE

from CASINO ROYALE

Words and Music by HAL DAVID
and BURT BACHARACH

Medium Rock Ballad, with much feeling

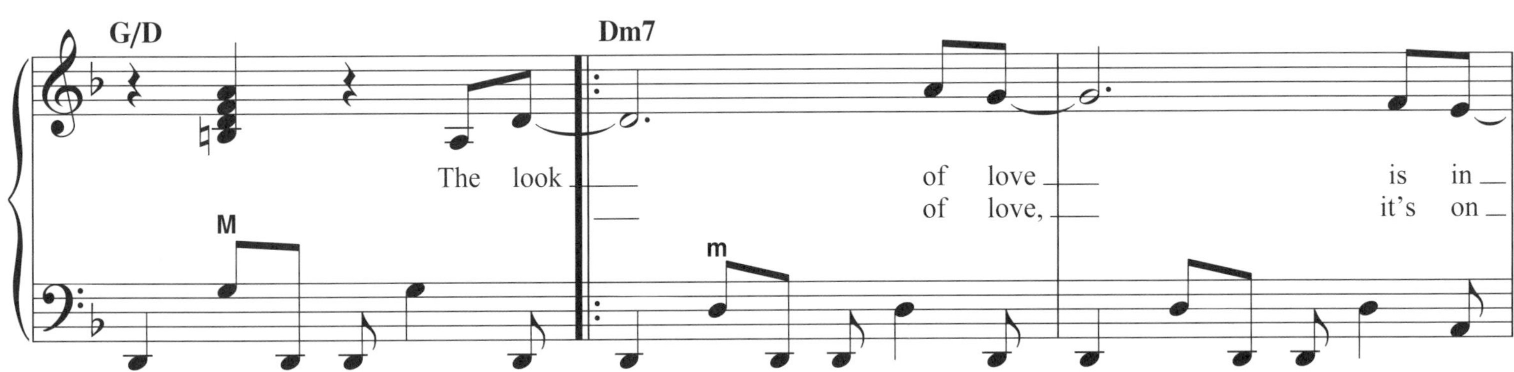

Bb6
A7sus
A7
can't dis - guise.
can't e - rase.
The look
Be mine
M
7
Dm7
D7
Bb6
of love,
to - night,
it's say - ing so
let this be just
m
7
M
Bbm6
F
F7
much more than just
the start of so
words could ev - er say.
man - y nights like this.
m
M
7
Bbmaj7
Bb6
A7sus
A7
And what my heart has heard, well, it
Let's take a lov - er's vow and then
takes my breath a - way.
seal it with a kiss.
M
M
7

Dm7
G7
F
Gm7
I can hard - ly wait to hold you, feel my arms a-round you, how long
f
m
M
M
m

F
Gm7
I have wait - ed, wait - ed just to love you. Now that I have found you,
M
m

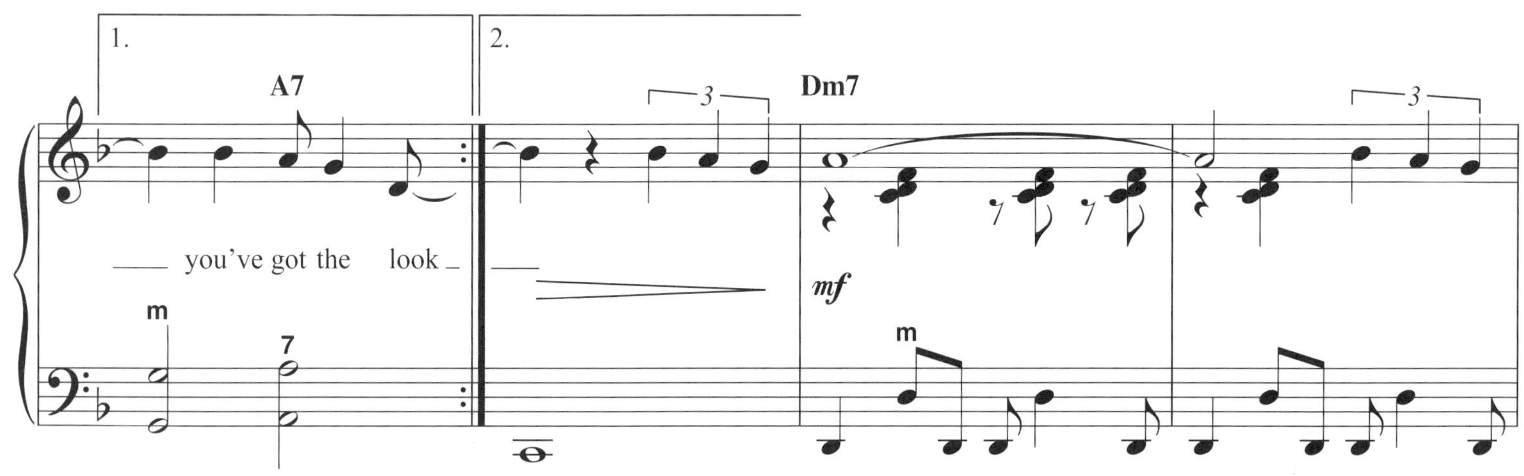
1.
2.
A7
Dm7
3
you've got the look
mf
m
7
m

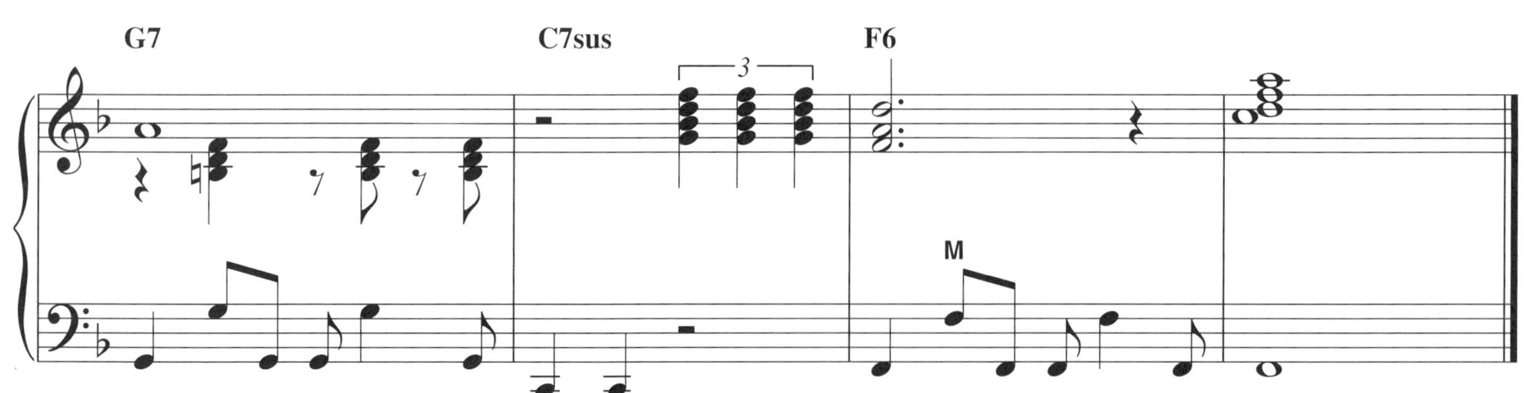
G7
C7sus
F6
3
M

MY HEART WILL GO ON

(Love Theme From 'Titanic')

from the Paramount and Twentieth Century Fox Motion Picture TITANIC

Music by JAMES HORNER
Lyric by WILL JENNINGS

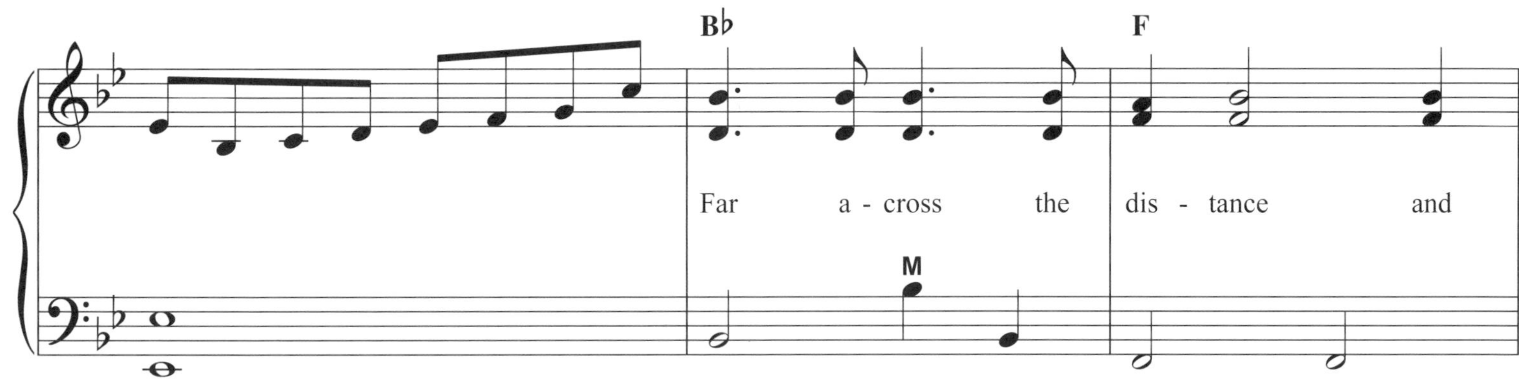
B♭
F
Far a - cross the dis - tance and
M

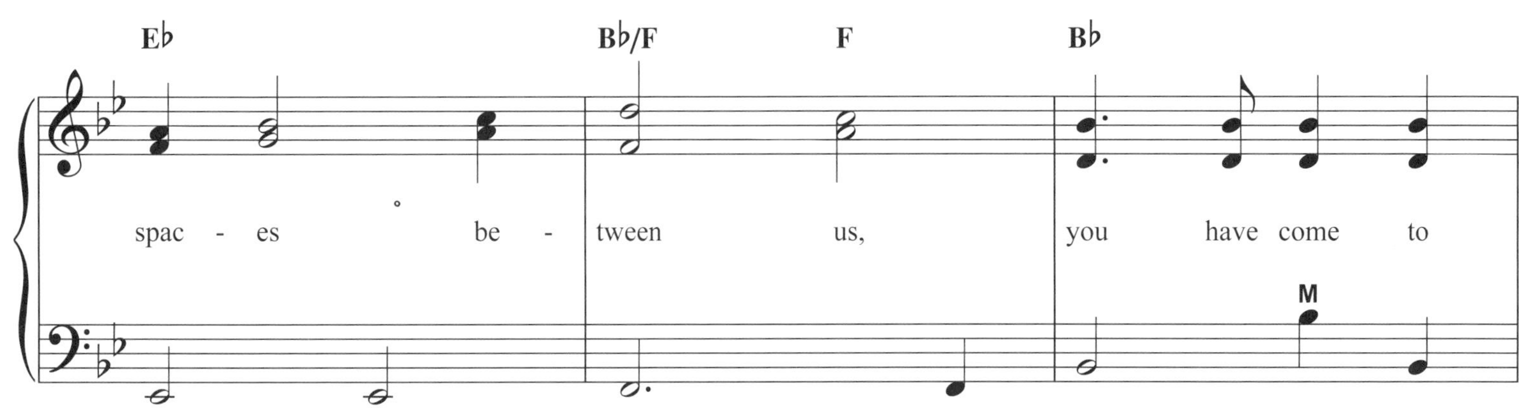
E♭
B♭/F
F
B♭
spac - es be - tween us,
you have come to
M

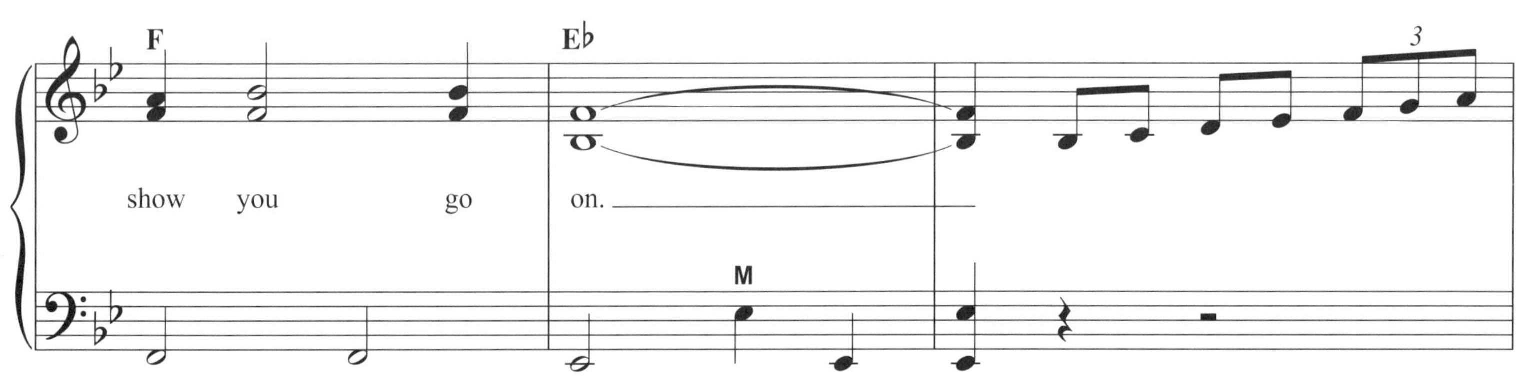
F
E♭
3
show you go
on.
M

Gm
F
E♭
Near,
far, wher -
ev - er you are,
m
M
M

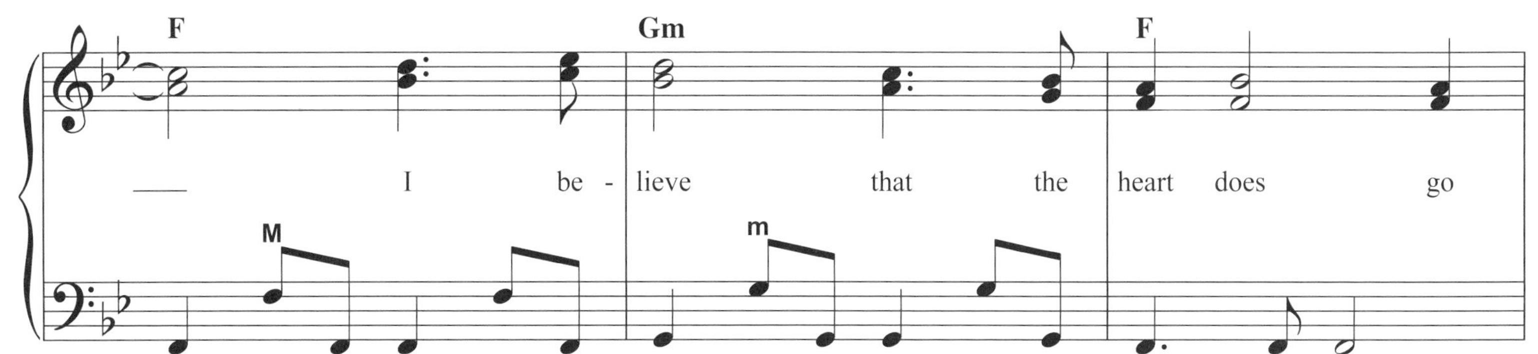
F
Gm
F
I be - lieve that the heart does go
M
m

E♭
F
Gm
on.
Once
M
m

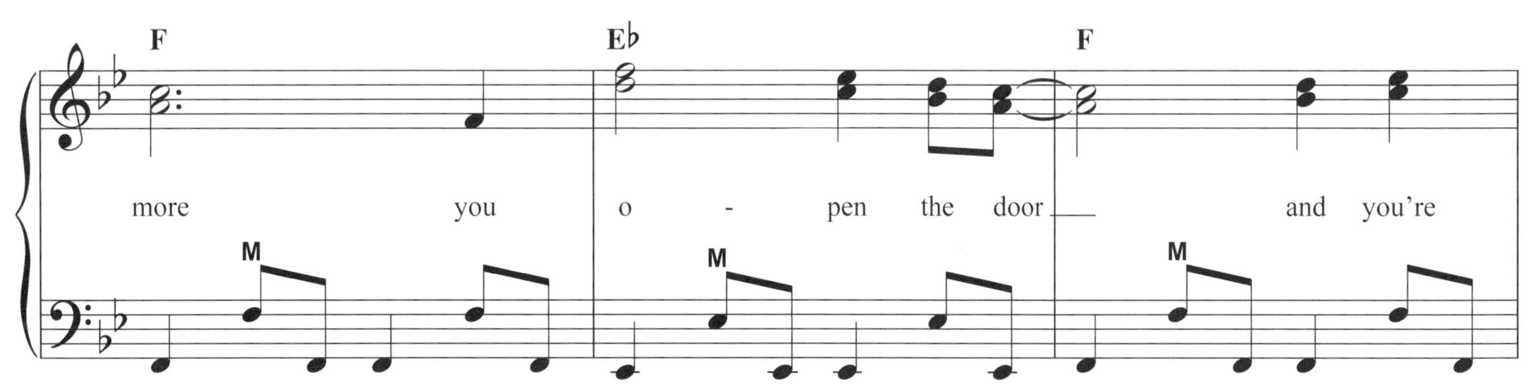
F
E♭
F
more you o - pen the door and you're
M
M
M

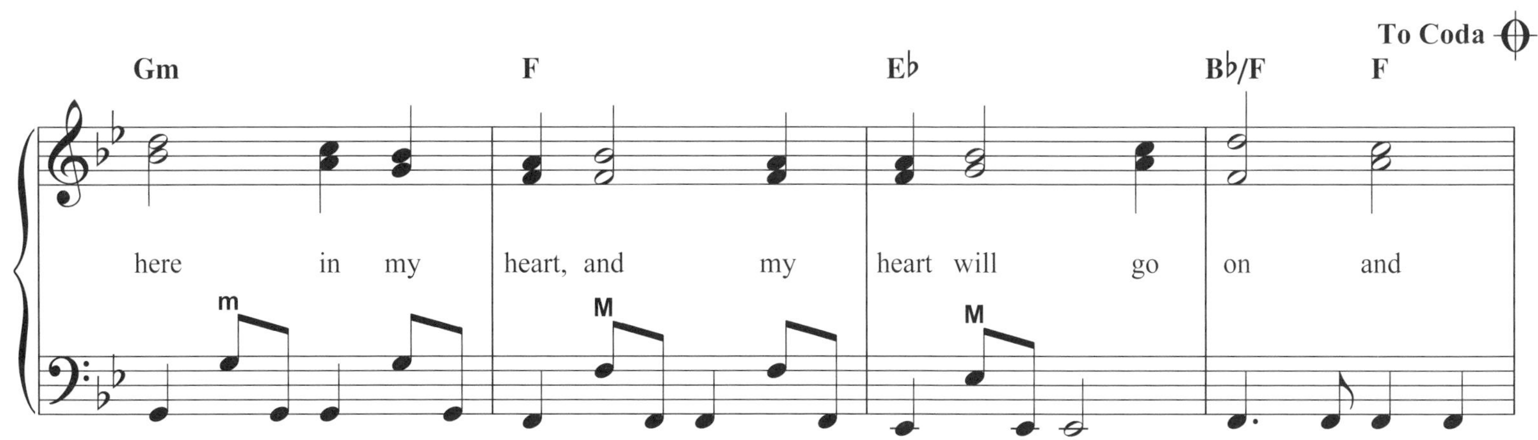
To Coda
Gm
F
E♭
B♭/F
F
here in my heart, and my heart will go on and
m
M
M

Gm
F
E♭
F
on.
(Instrumental)
m
M
M
M

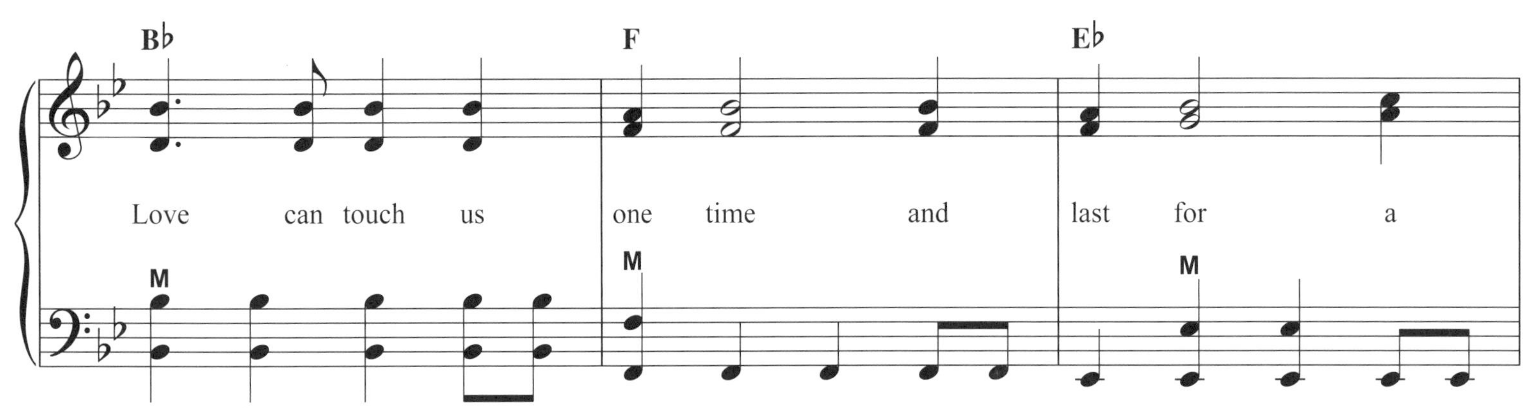
B♭
F
E♭
Love can touch us
one time and
last for a
M
M
M

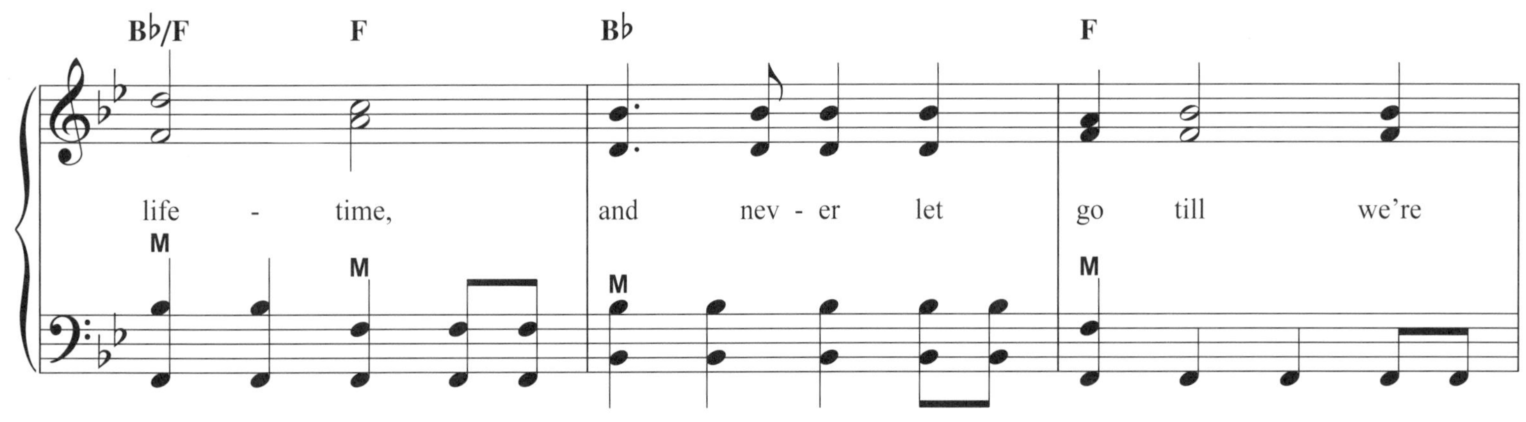
B♭/F
F
B♭
F
life - time,
and nev - er let
go till we're
M
M
M
M

E♭
B♭
gone.
Love was when I
M
M

F
E♭
B♭/F
D7/F♯
loved you; one true time I hold to.
M
M

Gm
Dm
E♭
In my life we'll al - ways go on.
m
m
M

D.S. al Coda

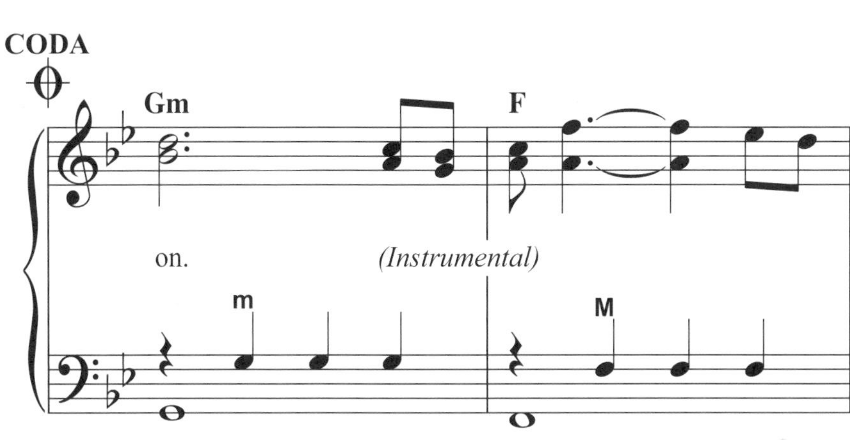
CODA
Gm
F
on.
(Instrumental)
m
M

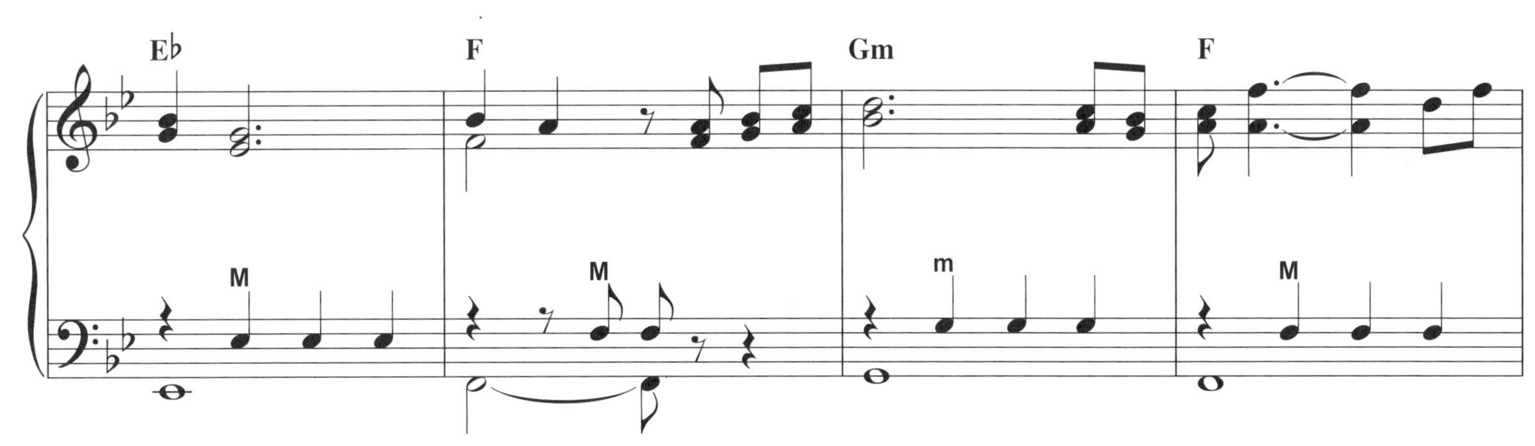
E♭
F
Gm
F
M
M
m
M

E♭
Gm/D
D7
Bm
A
You're here, there's
M
m
M

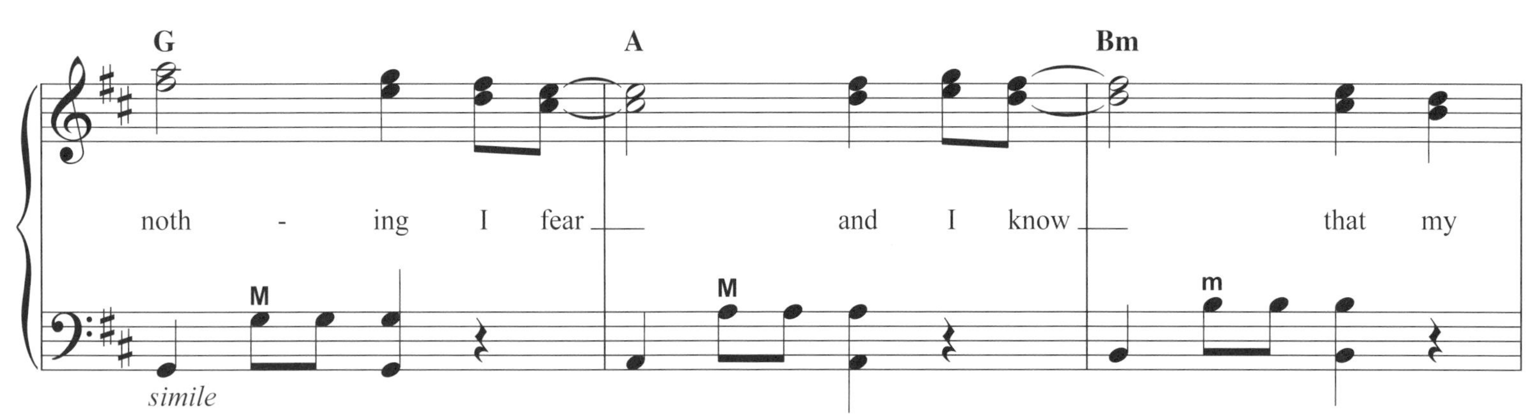
G
A
Bm
noth - ing I fear and I know that my
M
M
m
simile

A
G
A
heart will go on.
M
M

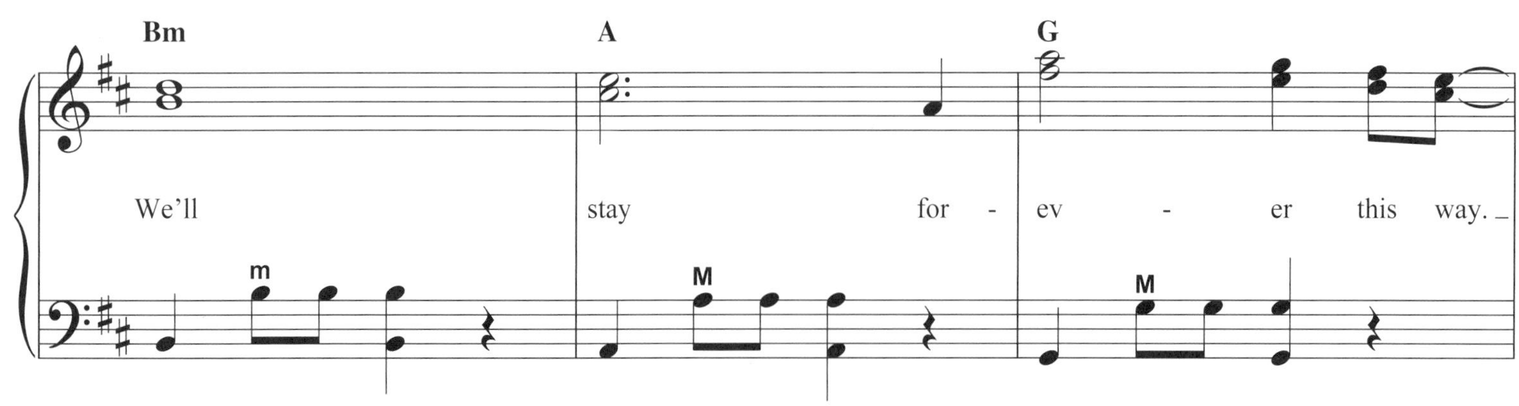
Bm
A
G
We'll stay for - ev - er this way.
m
M
M

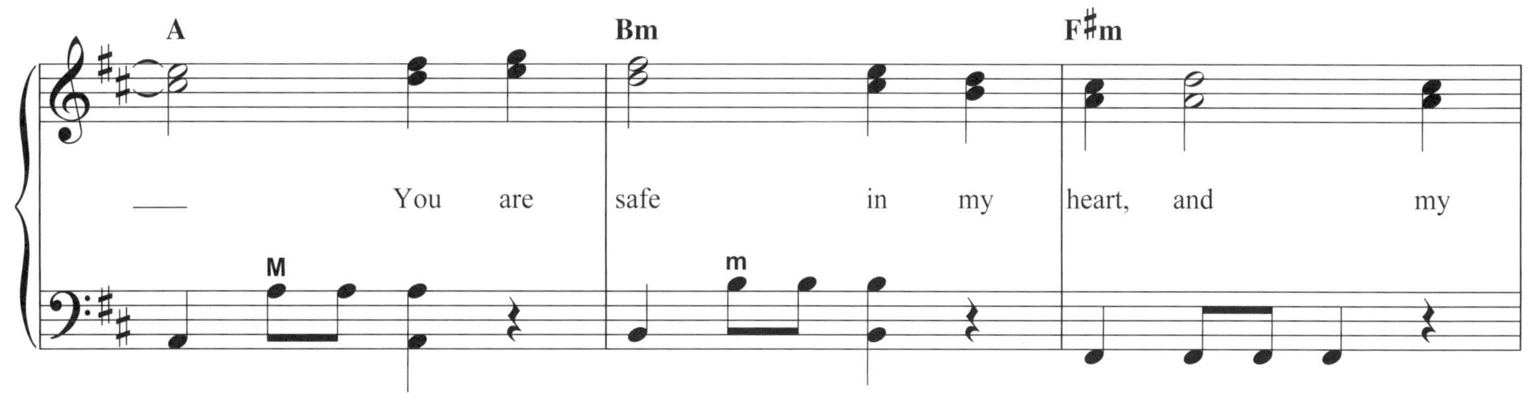
A
Bm
F♯m
You are safe in my heart, and my
M
m

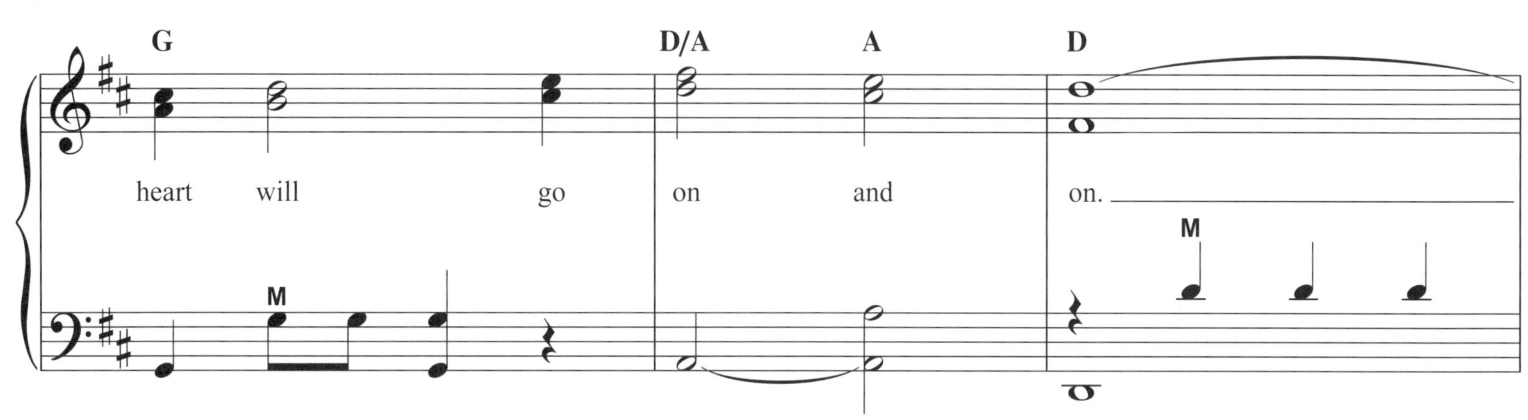
G
D/A
A
D
heart will go on and on.
M
M

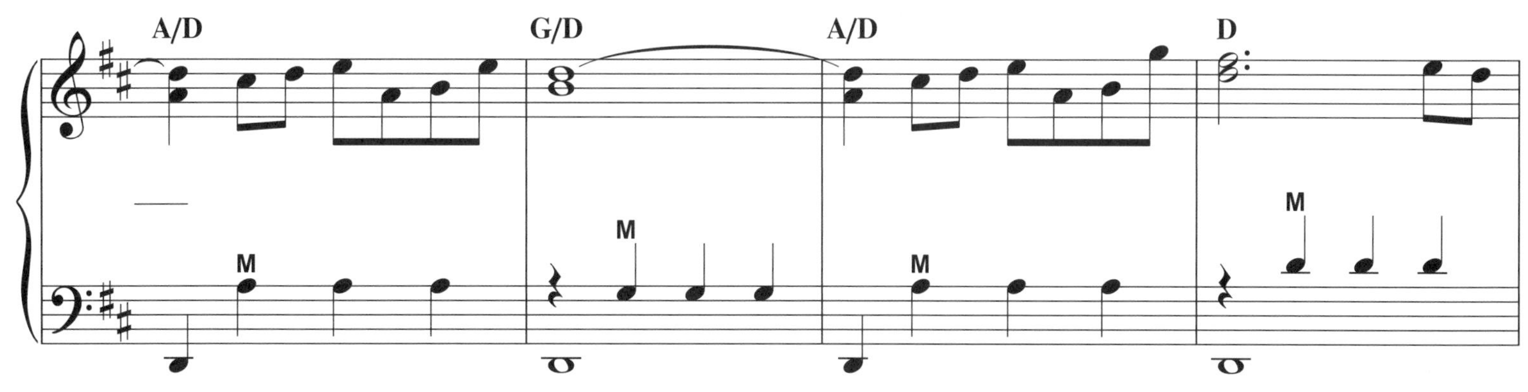
A/D
G/D
A/D
D
M
M
M
M

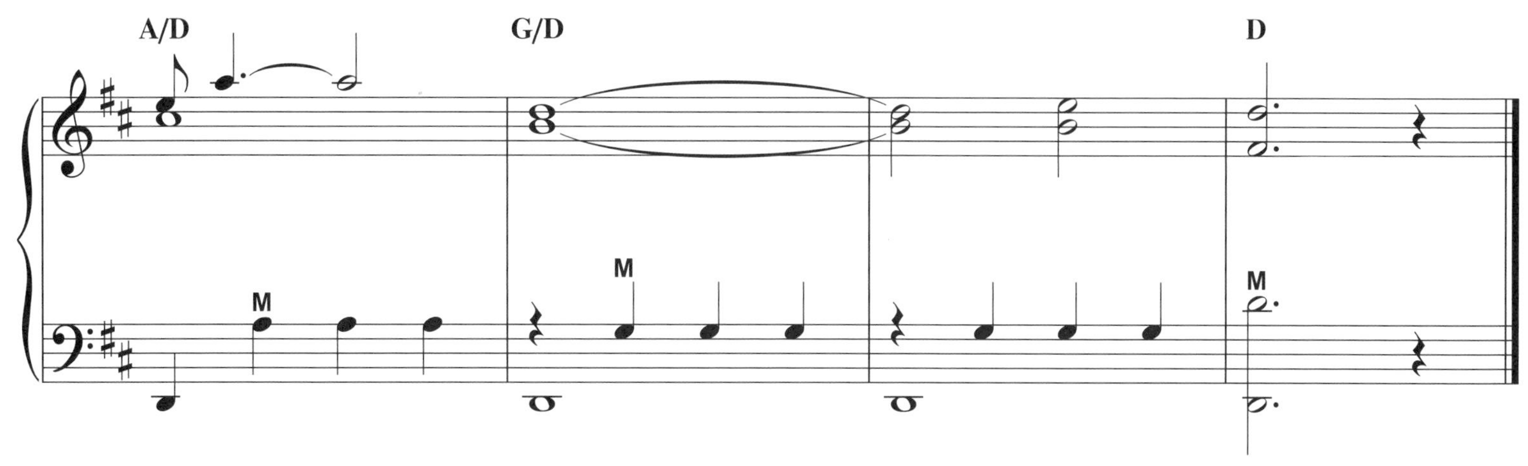
A/D
G/D
D
M
M
M

MIA & SEBASTIAN'S THEME

from LA LA LAND

Music by
JUSTIN HURWITZ

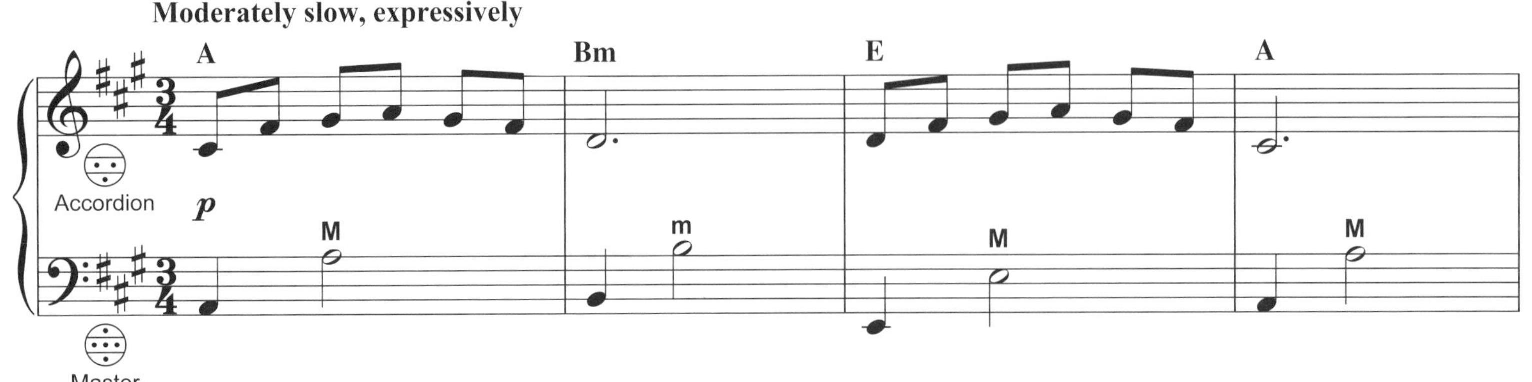

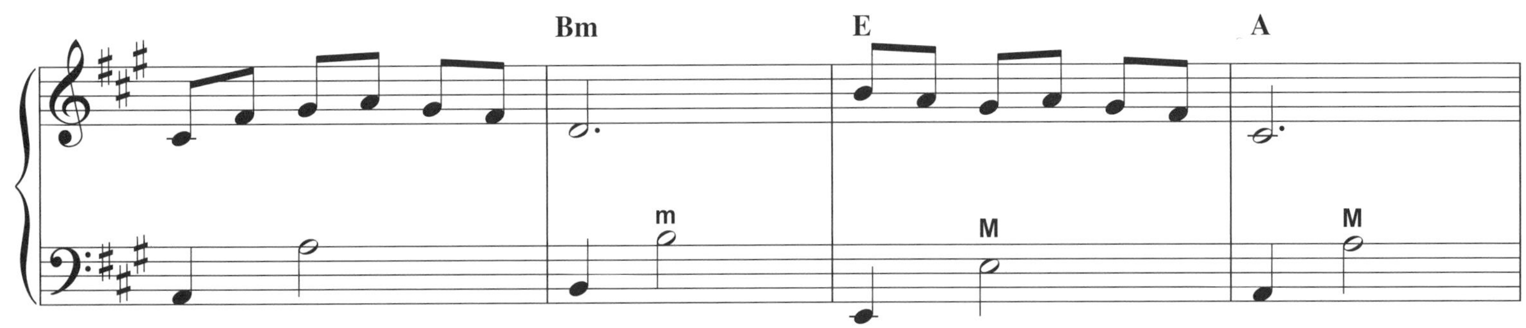

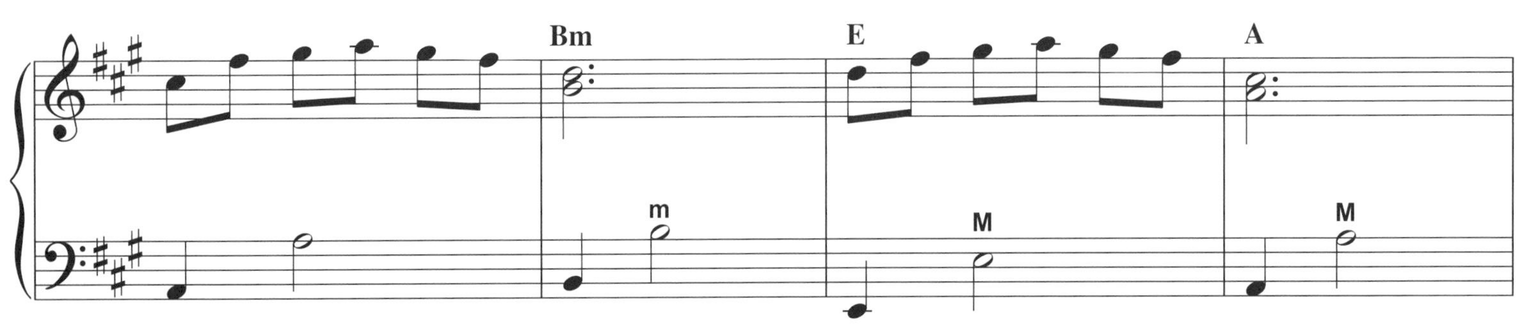

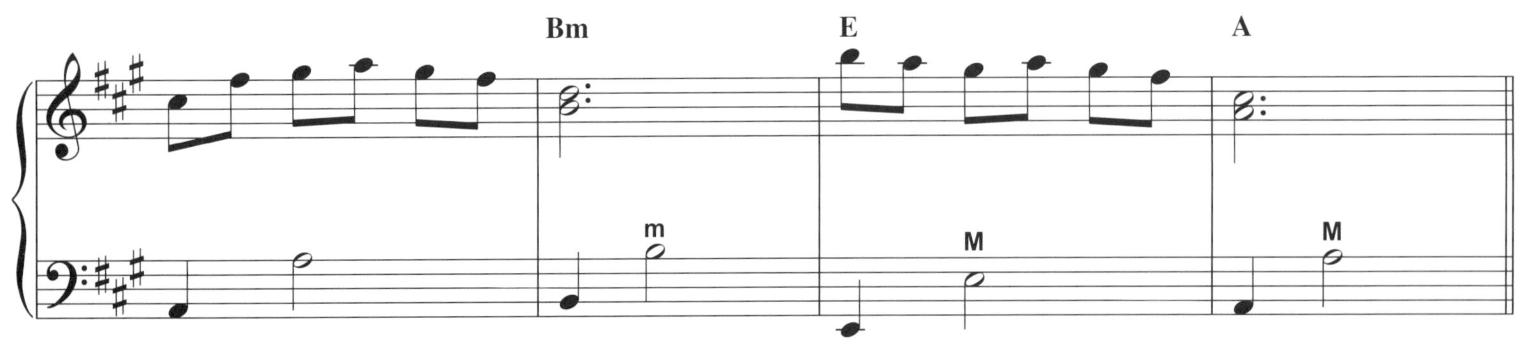

Bm
E
A
D
Bm
m
M
M
M
m

E
A
Bm
E
M
M
m
M

C♯7
F♯m
D
F♯m/C♯
7
m
M
m

Cdim
C♯
F♯m
rit.
pp
dim
M
m

A MILLION DREAMS

from THE GREATEST SHOWMAN

Words and Music by BENJ PASEK
and JUSTIN PAUL

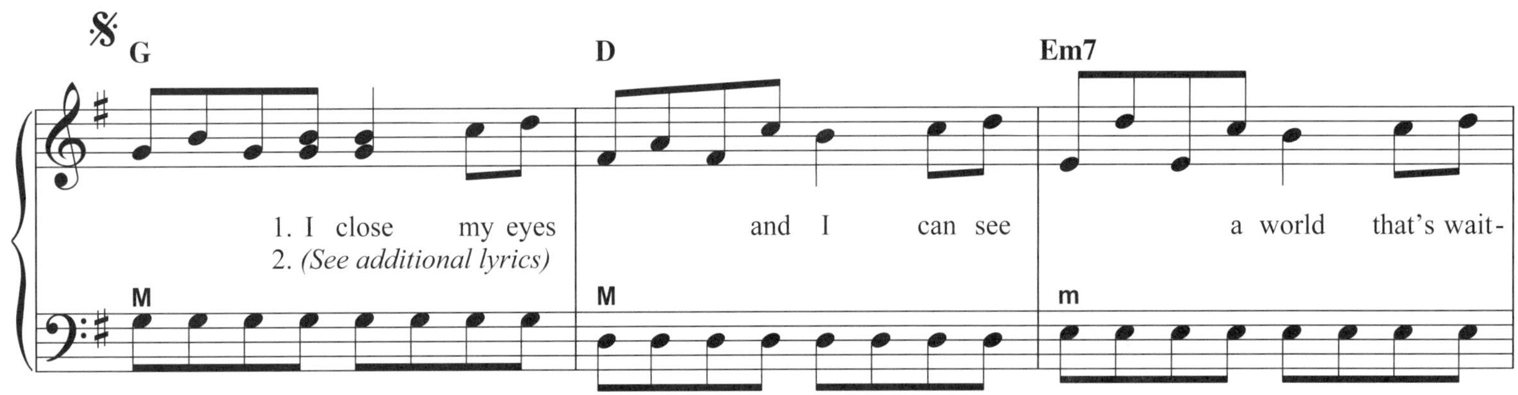

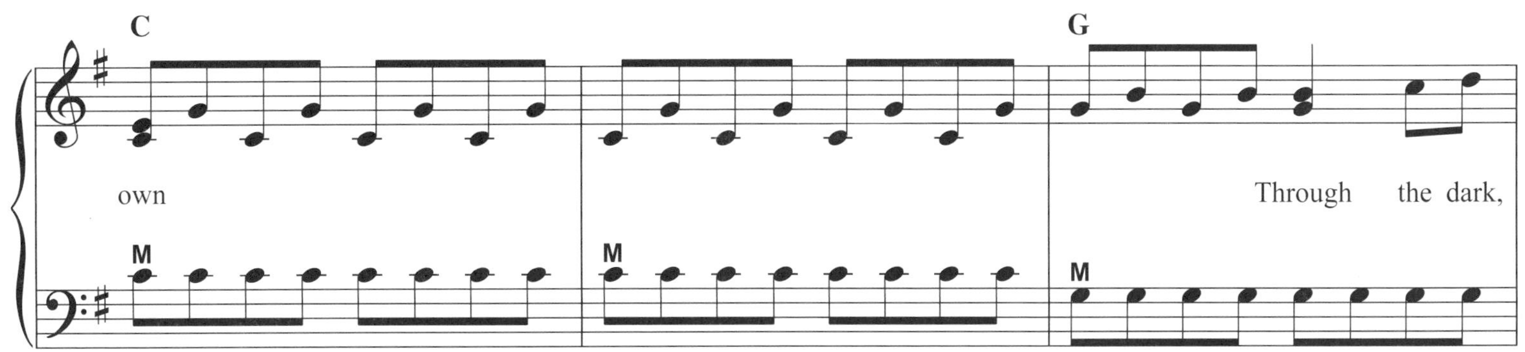
C
G
own
Through the dark,
M
M
M

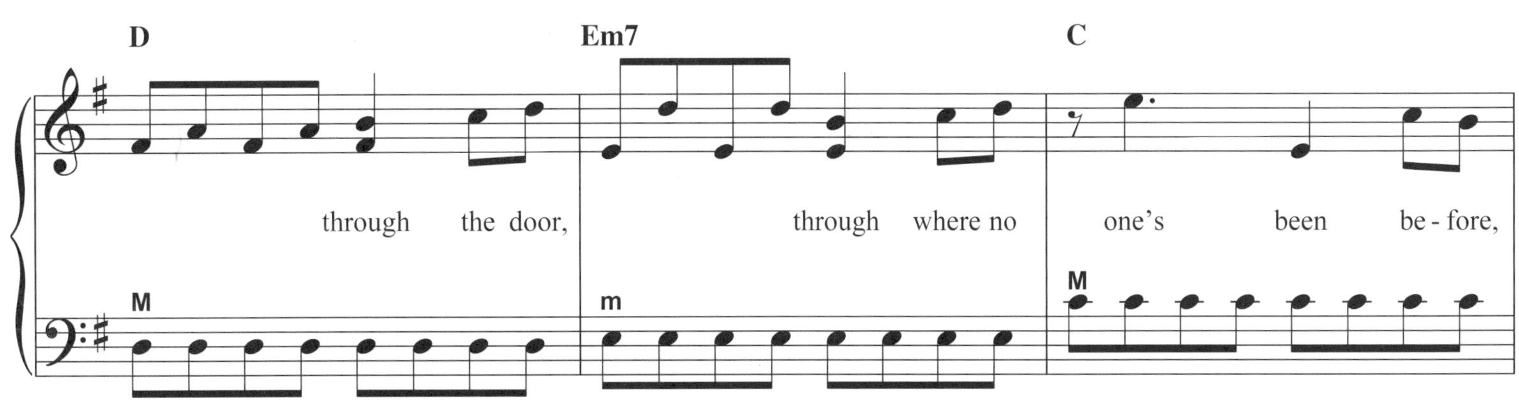
D
Em7
C
through the door,
through where no
one's been be - fore,
M
m
M

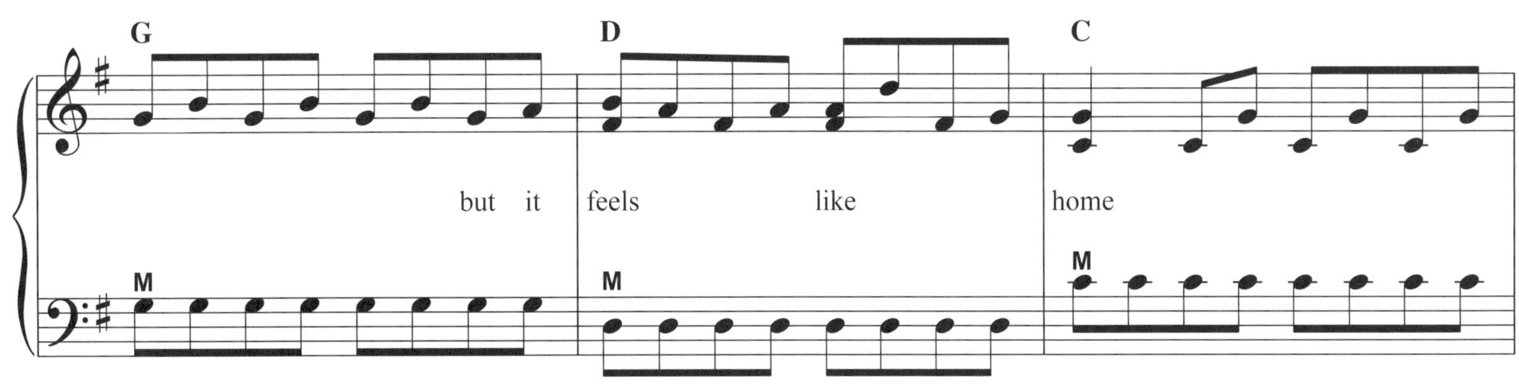
G
D
C
but it
feels like
home
M
M
M

Pre-Chorus
D
Em
They can say, they can
say it all ___ sounds cra -
M
m

C
D
M
M
- zy
They can say, they can
They can say, they can

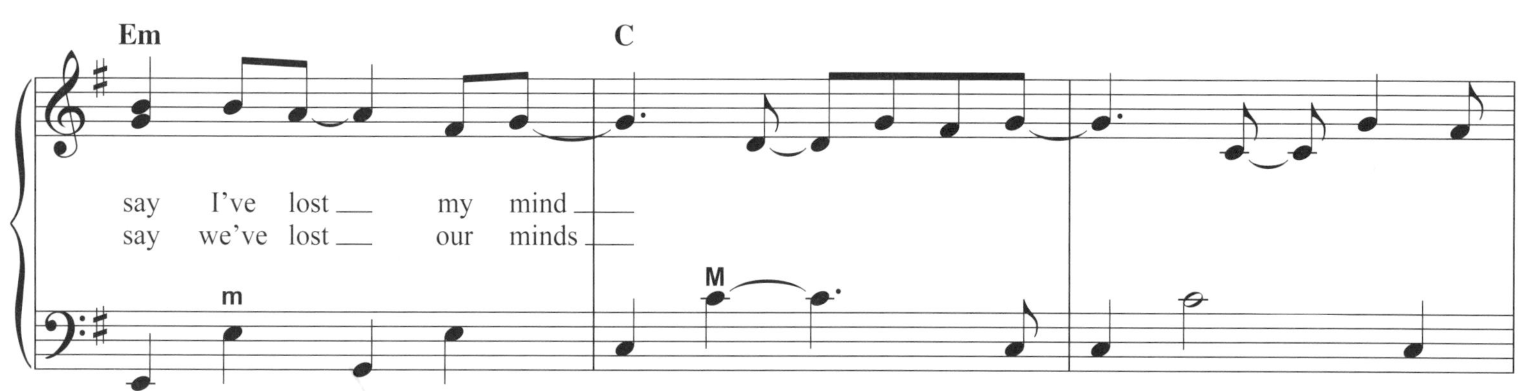
Em
C
m
M
say I've lost my mind
say we've lost our minds

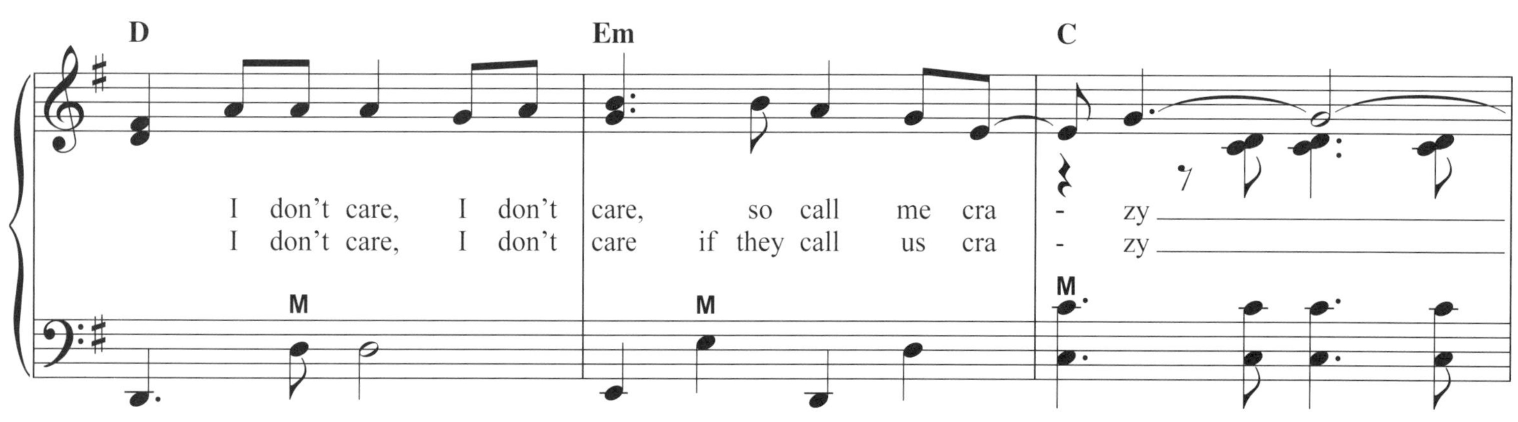
D
Em
C
M
M
M
I don't care, I don't care, so call me cra - zy
I don't care, I don't care if they call us cra - zy

D
Em
M
m
We can live in a world that we de - sign
Run a - way to a world that we de - sign

C
G
'Cause
ev - 'ry night I lie
mf
M
M

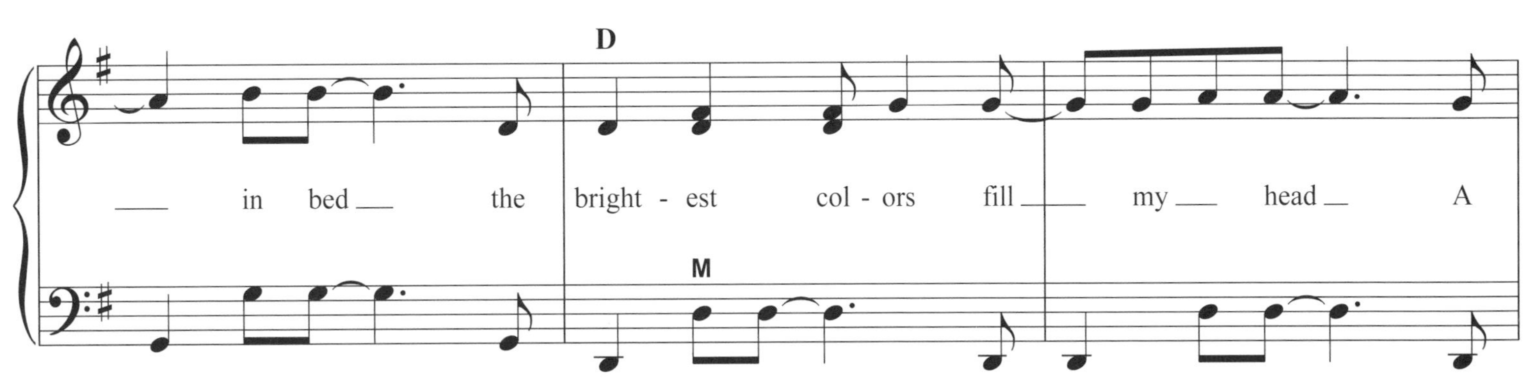
D
in bed the
bright - est col - ors fill
my head A
M

Am
C
mil - lion dreams are keep
- in' me a - wake
m
M

G
I
think of what the world
could be, a
M

D
Am
vi - sion of the one I see A mil - lion dreams is all
M
m

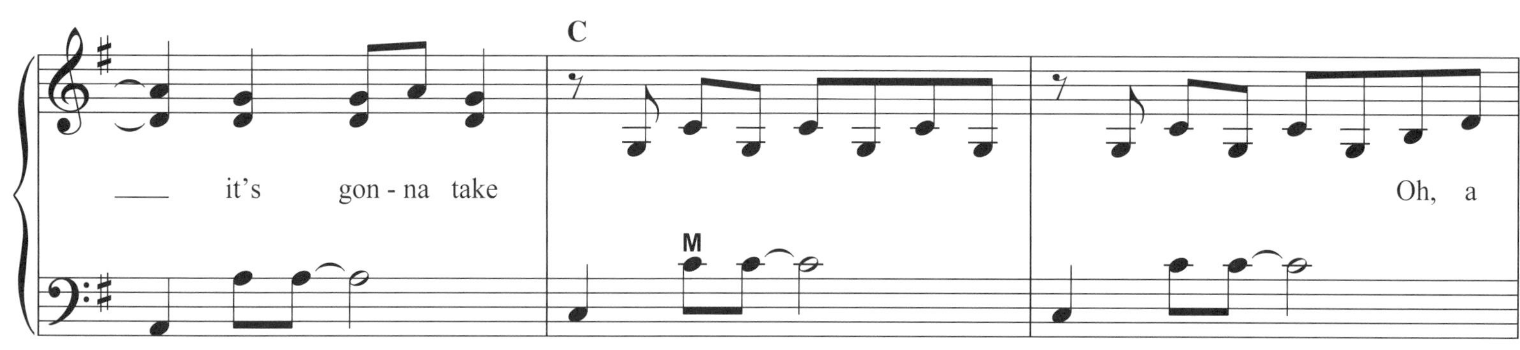
C
it's gon - na take
Oh, a
M

To Coda
G
mil - lion dreams for the world we're gon - na make

D
Em7
C
D.S. al Coda

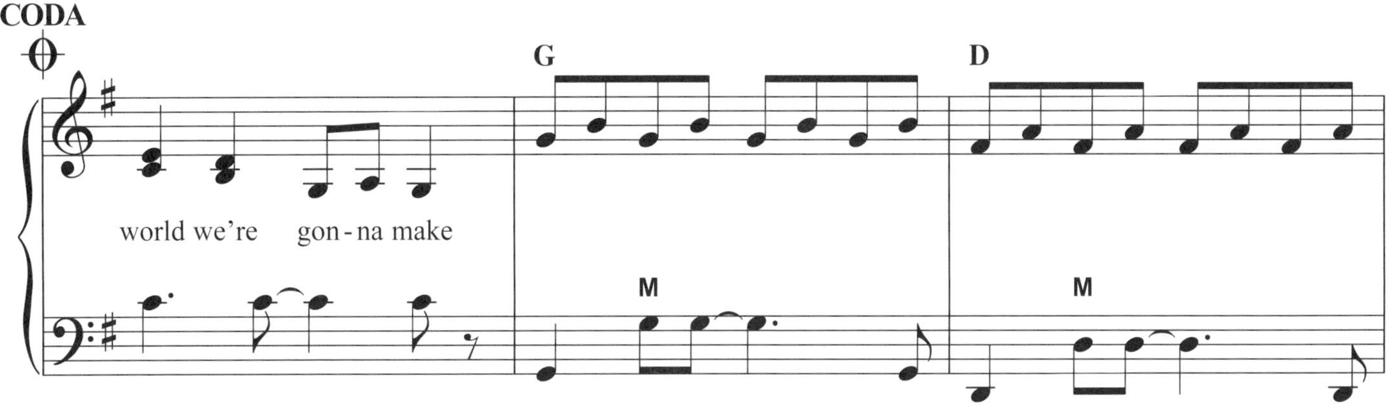

Additional Lyrics

2. There's a house we can build
   Ev'ry room inside is filled with things from far away
   Special things I compile,
   Each one there to make you smile on a rainy day
   (Pre-Chorus)

MRS. ROBINSON
from THE GRADUATE

Words and Music by
PAUL SIMON

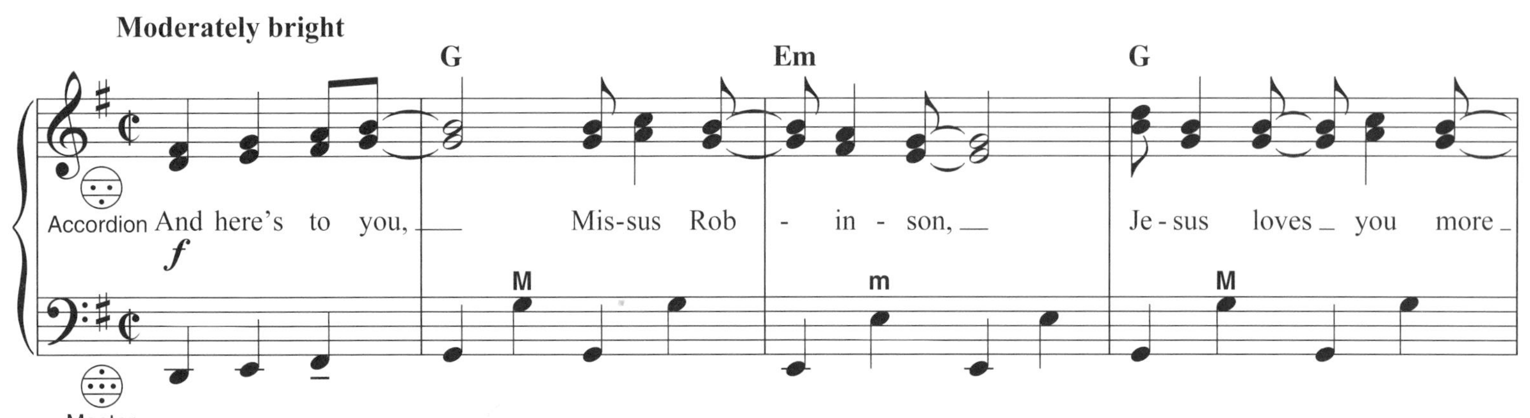

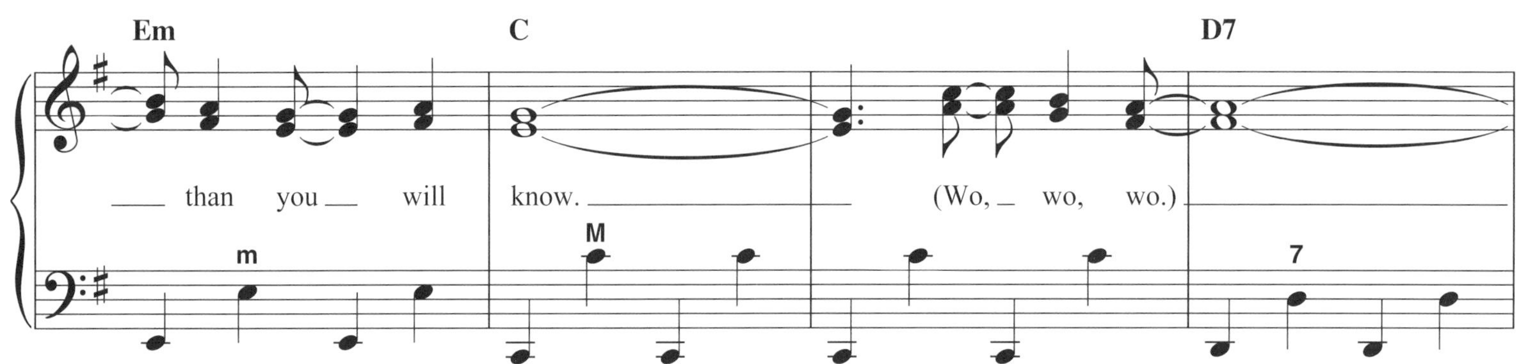

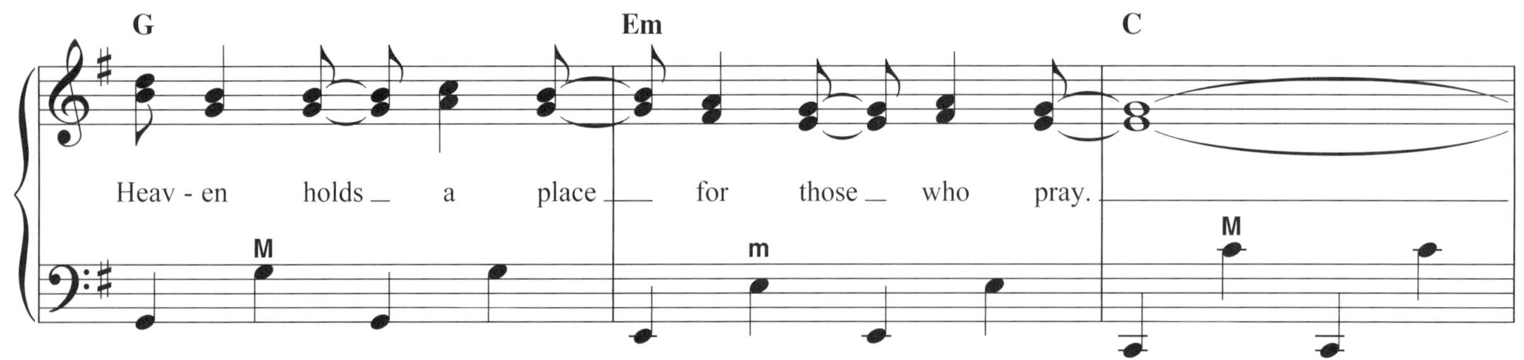

Am
E
(Hey, hey, hey,
hey, hey hey.)
m

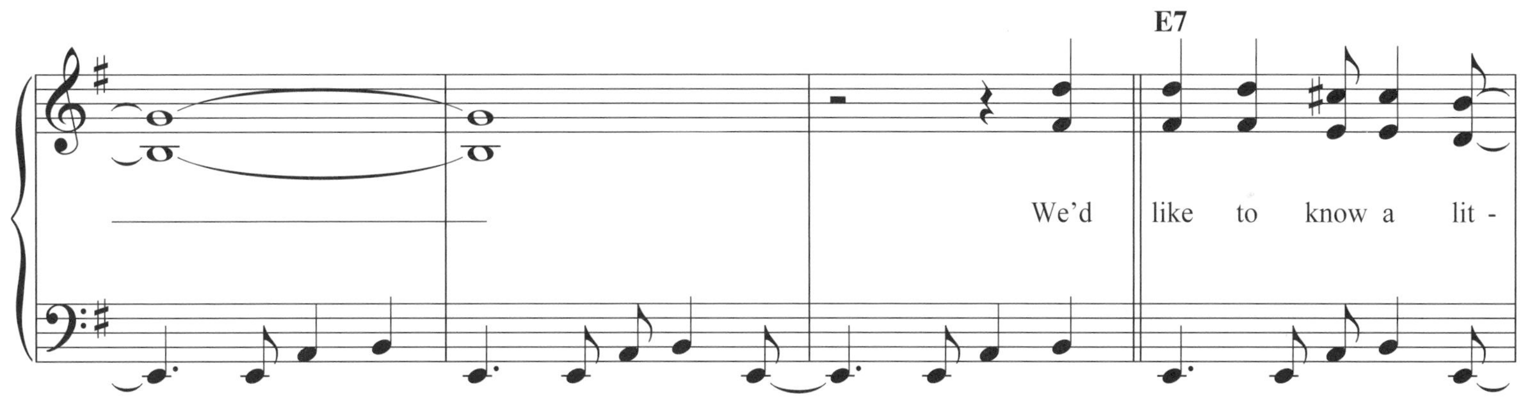
E7
We'd
like to know a lit -

- tle bit a - bout you for our files,
we'd

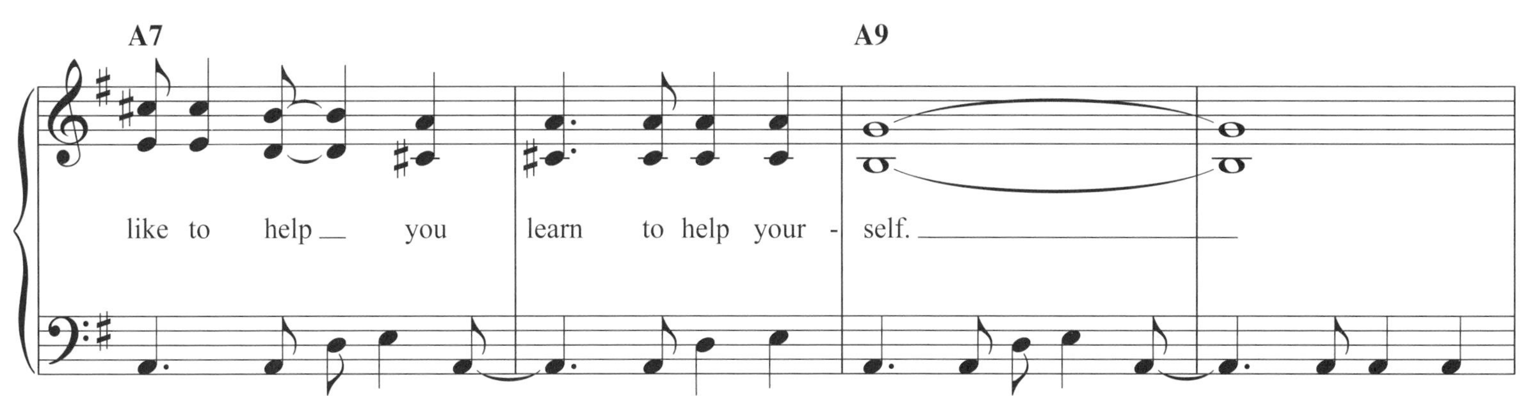
A7
A9
like to help you learn to help your - self.

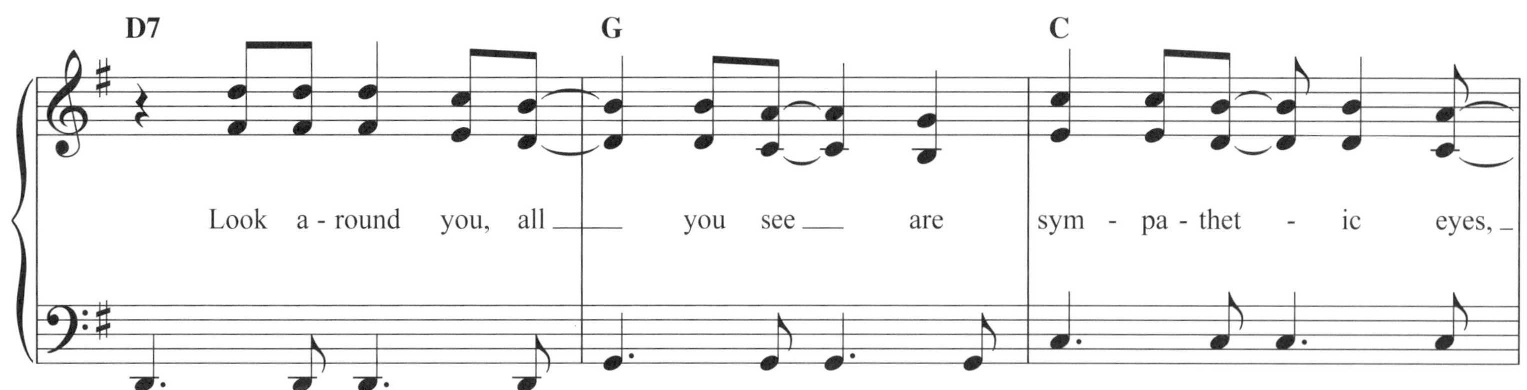
D7
G
C
Look a - round you, all you see are sym - pa - thet - ic eyes,

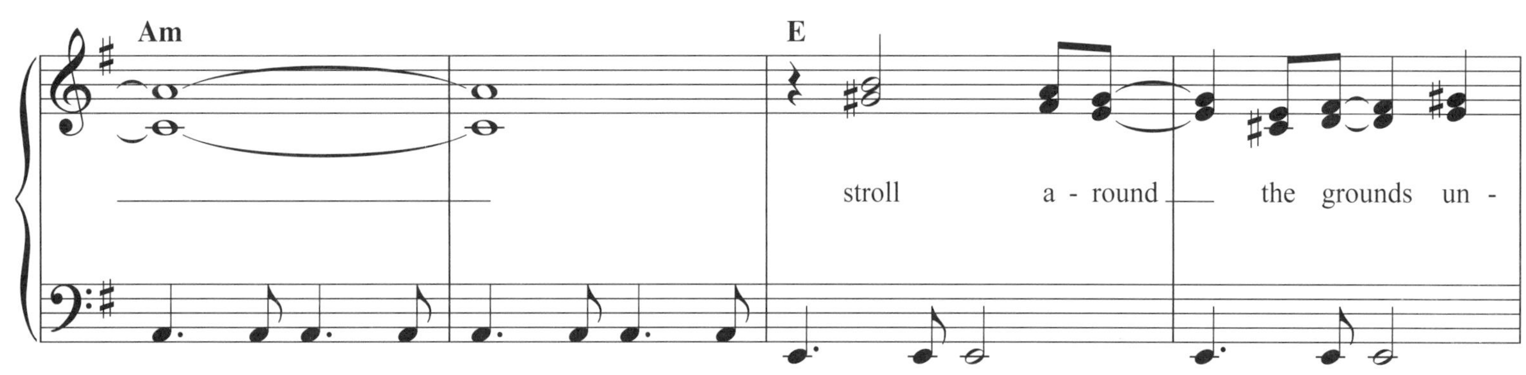
Am
E
stroll a - round the grounds un -

D7
G
til you feel at home. And here's to you, Mis - sus Rob -
M

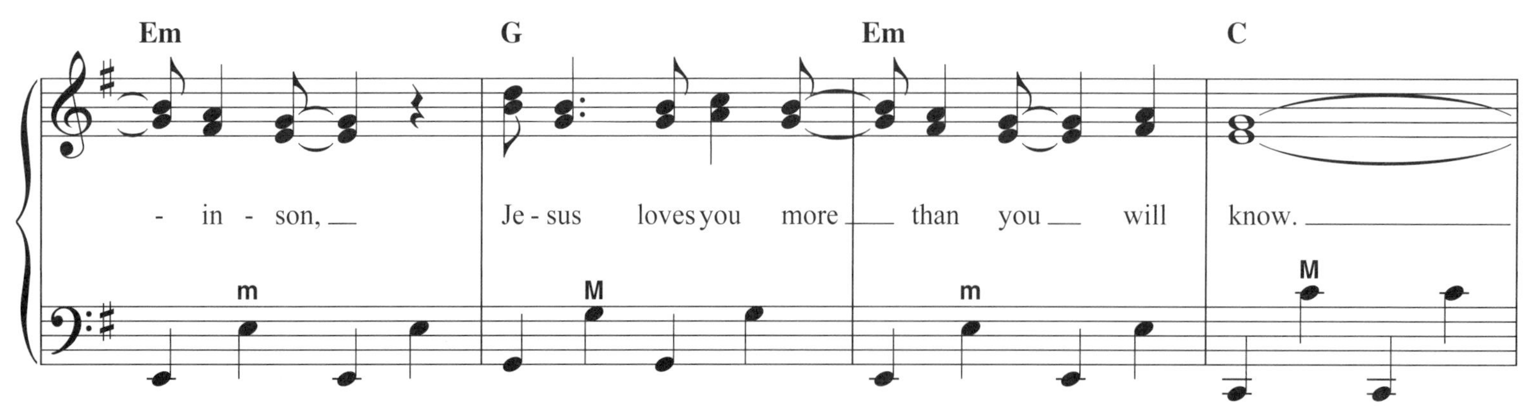
Em
G
Em
C
- in - son, Je - sus loves you more than you will know.
m
M
m
M

D7
G
(Wo, wo, wo.)
God bless you, please, Mis-sus Rob-
7
M

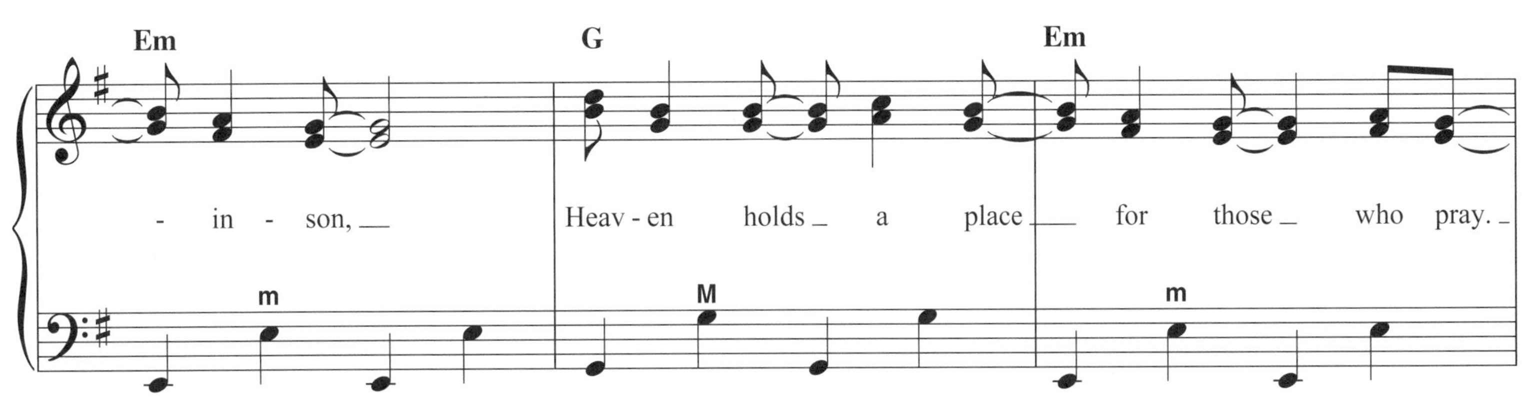
Em
G
Em
- in - son,
Heav - en holds a place for those who pray.
m
M
m

C
Am
(Hey, hey, hey,
hey, hey, hey.)
M
m

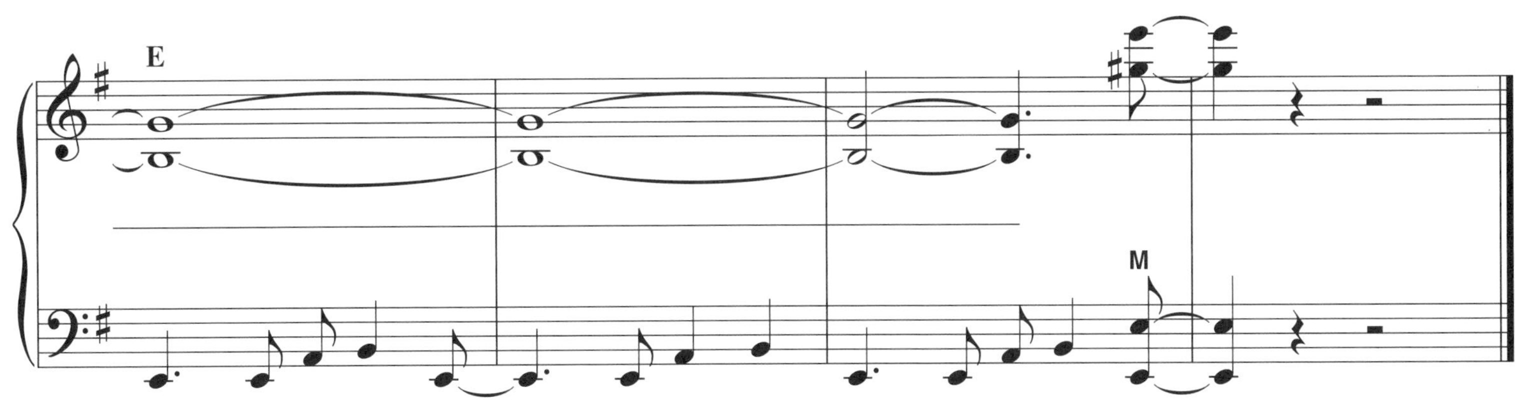
E
M

THEME FROM "NEW YORK, NEW YORK"

from NEW YORK, NEW YORK

Words by FRED EBB
Music by JOHN KANDER

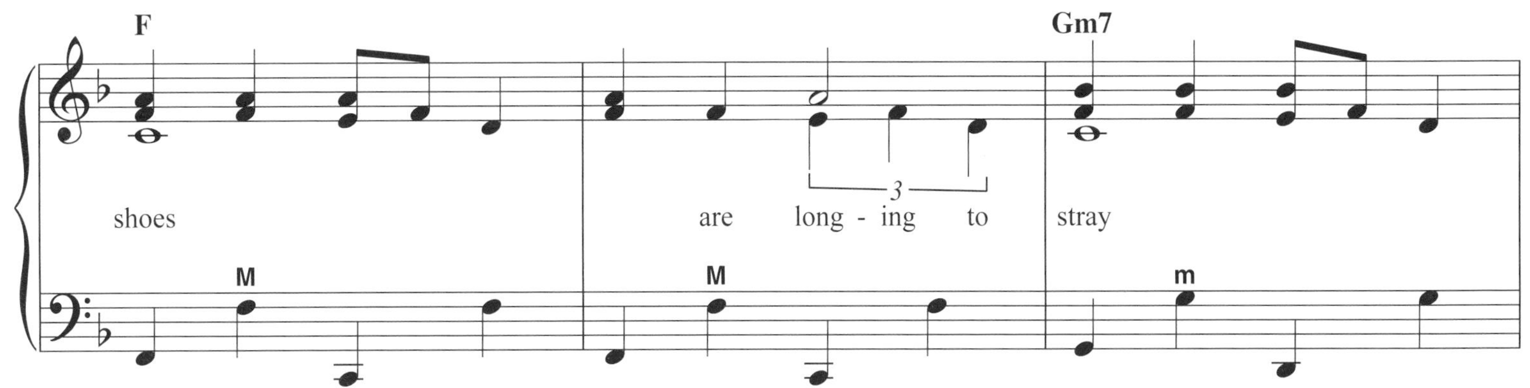
F
Gm7
shoes
are long - ing to
stray
M
M
m

C7
F
Fmaj7
and step a -
round the heart of it,
New York, New
M

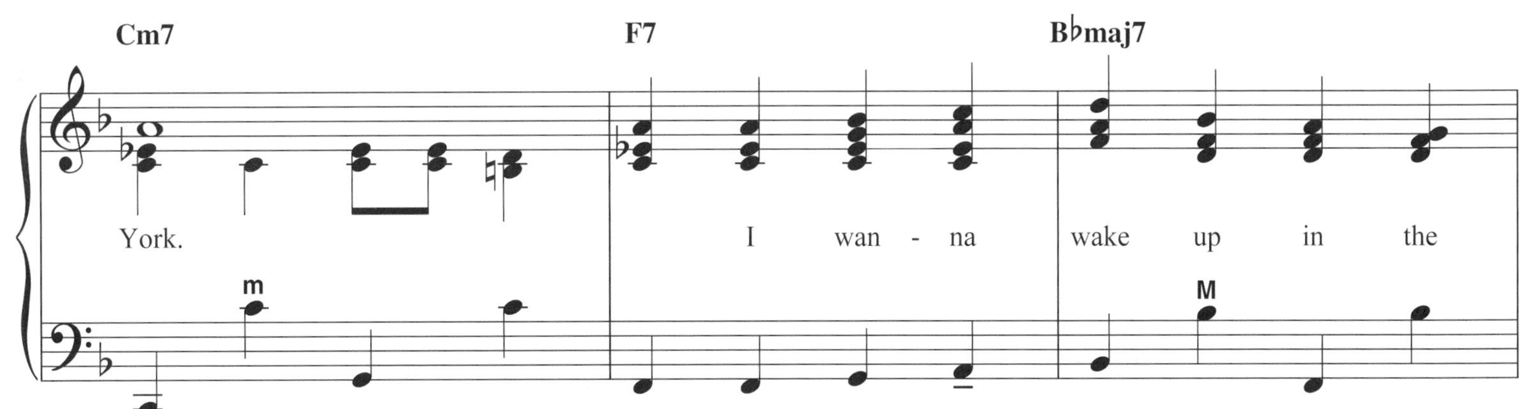
Cm7
F7
B♭maj7
York.
I wan - na
wake up in the
m
M

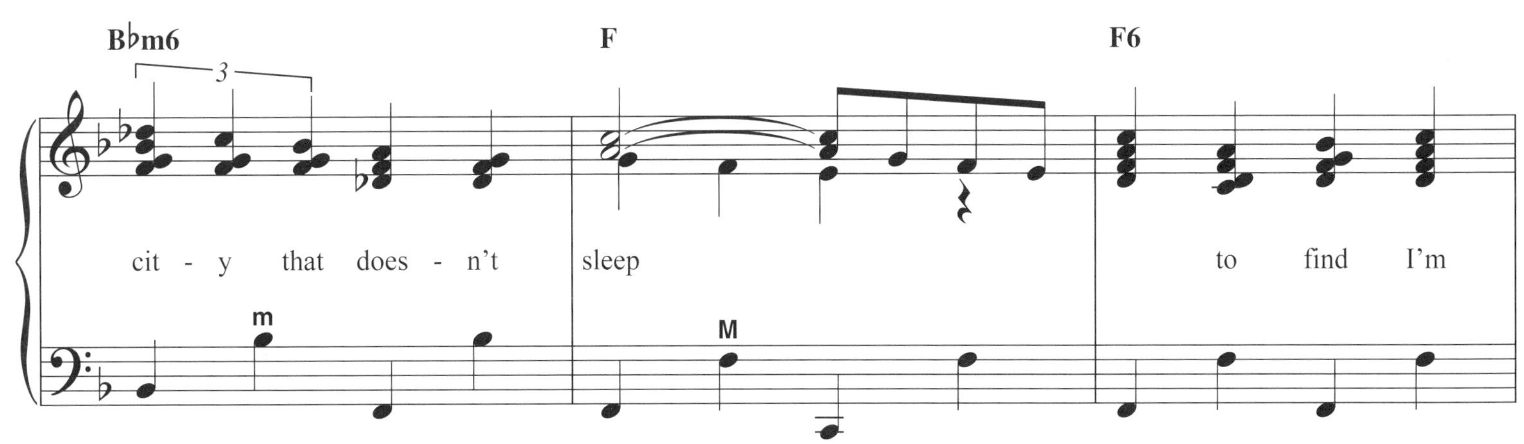
B♭m6
F
F6
cit - y that does - n't
sleep
to find I'm
m
M

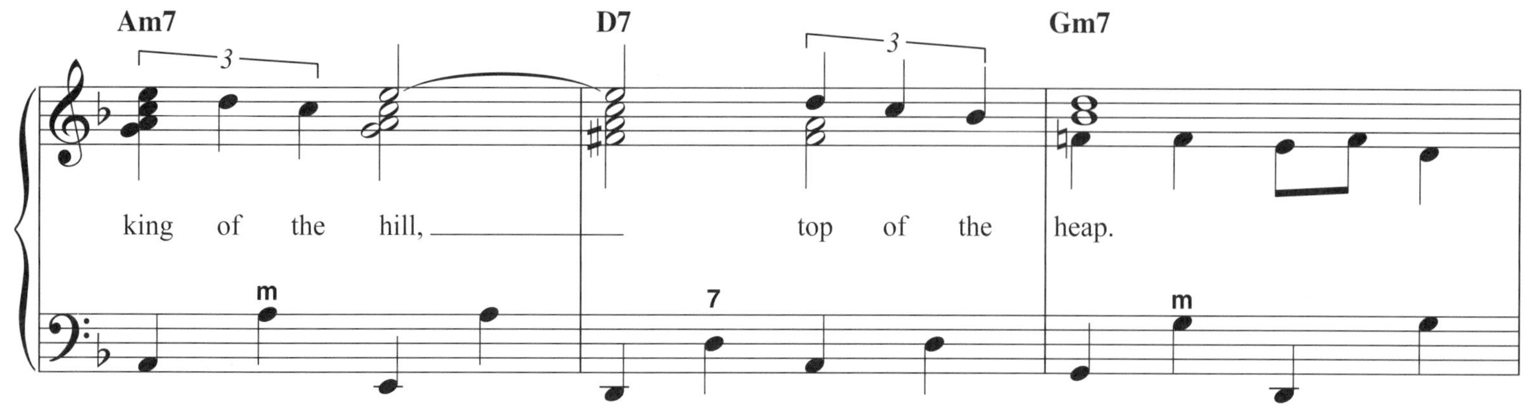
Am7
D7
Gm7
3
3
king of the hill,
top of the heap.
m
7
m

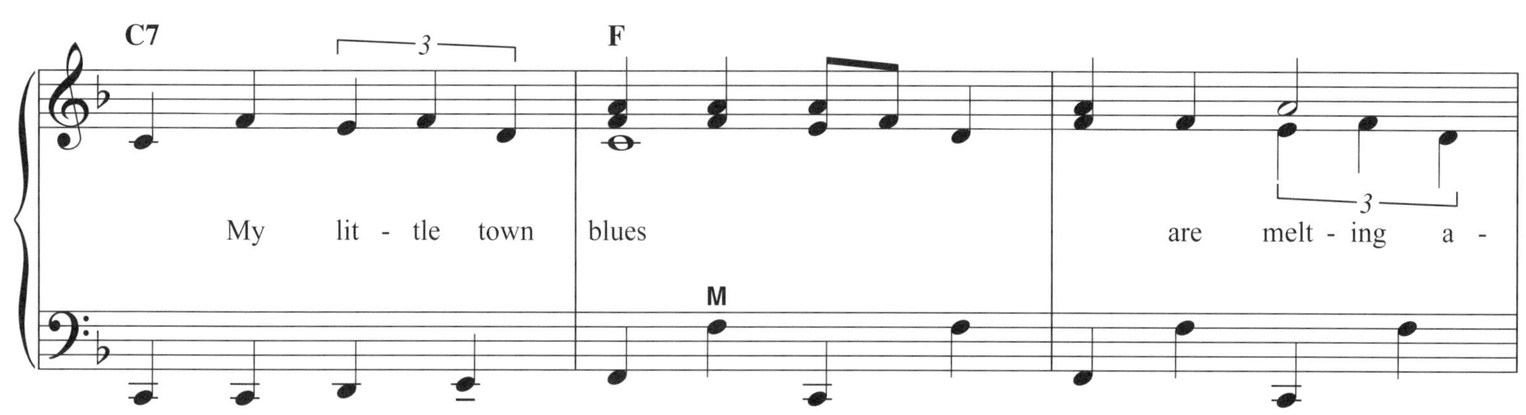
C7
F
3
3
My lit - tle town blues are melt - ing a -
M

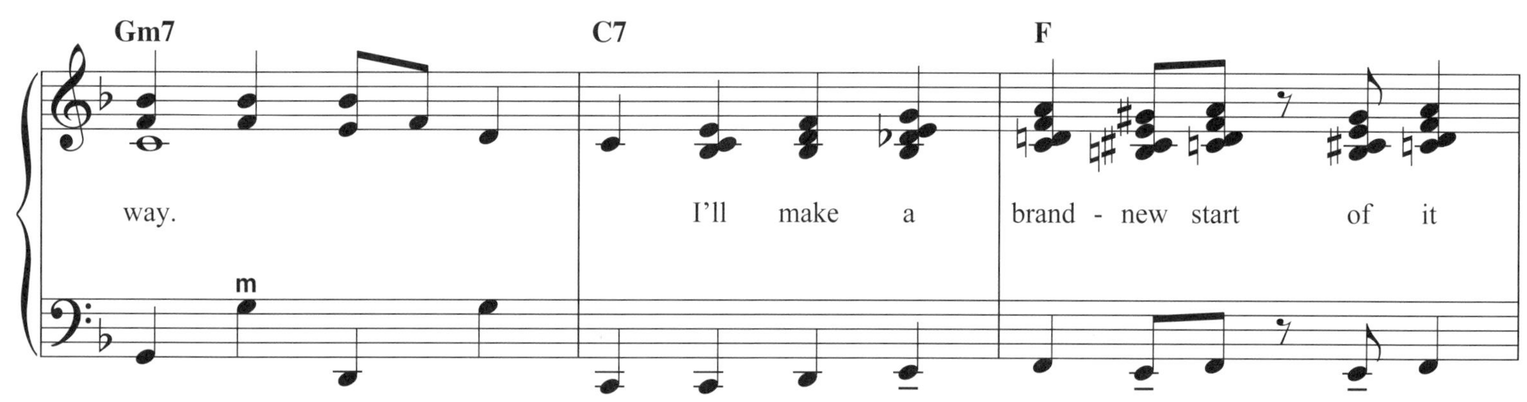
Gm7
C7
F
way. I'll make a brand - new start of it
m

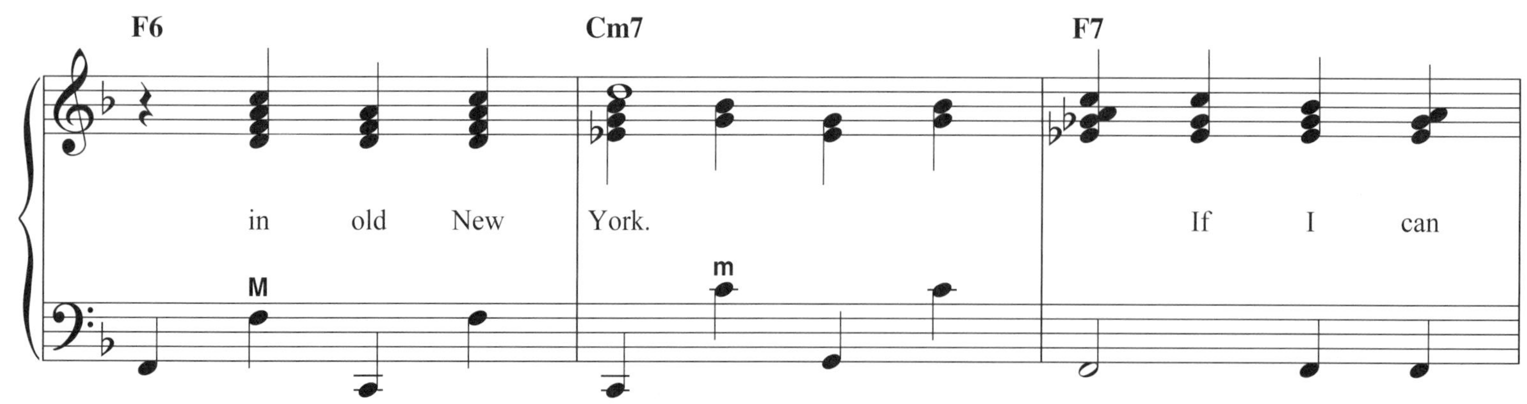
F6
Cm7
F7
in old New York. If I can
M
m

B♭
B♭m6
F
D7♯5
make it there, I'd make it an - y - where.
M
m
M

D7
Gm7
Am7
B♭maj7
C9sus
It's up to you, New York, New
7

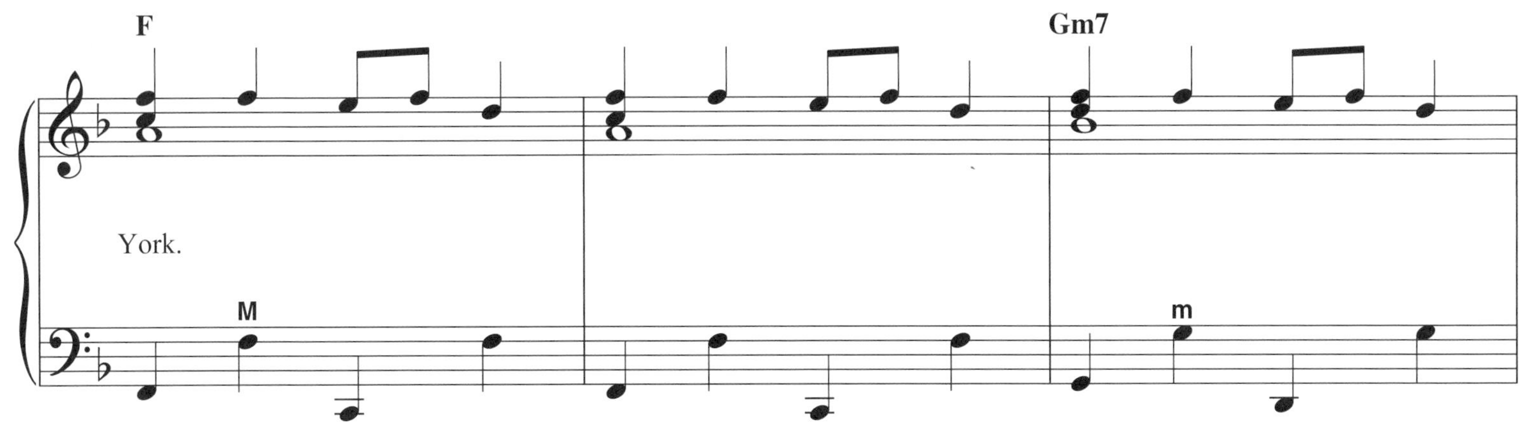
F
Gm7
York.
M
m

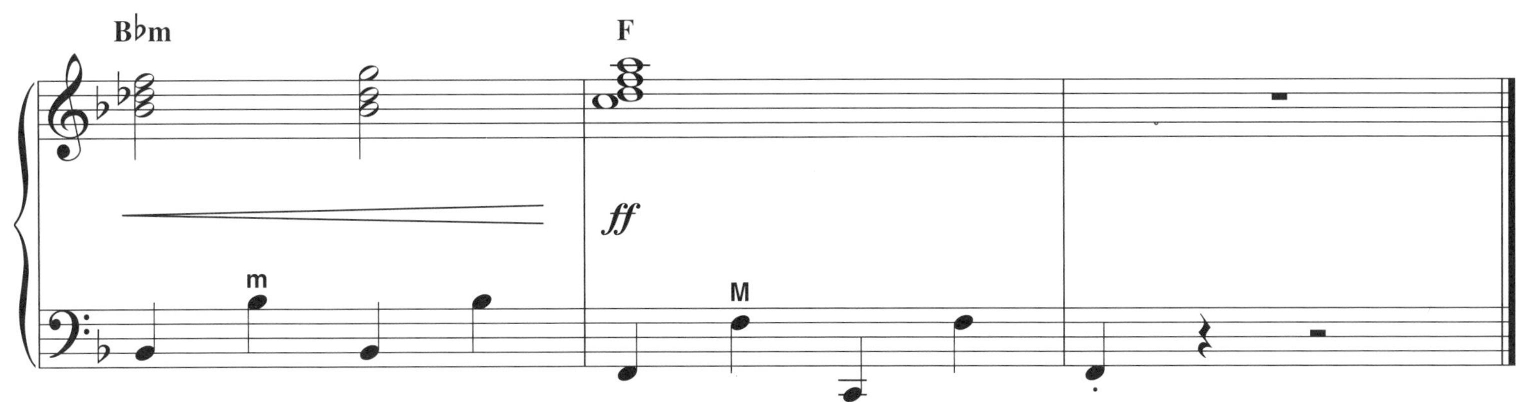
B♭m
F
ff
m
M

NOBODY DOES IT BETTER

from THE SPY WHO LOVED ME

Music by MARVIN HAMLISCH
Lyrics by CAROLE BAYER SAGER

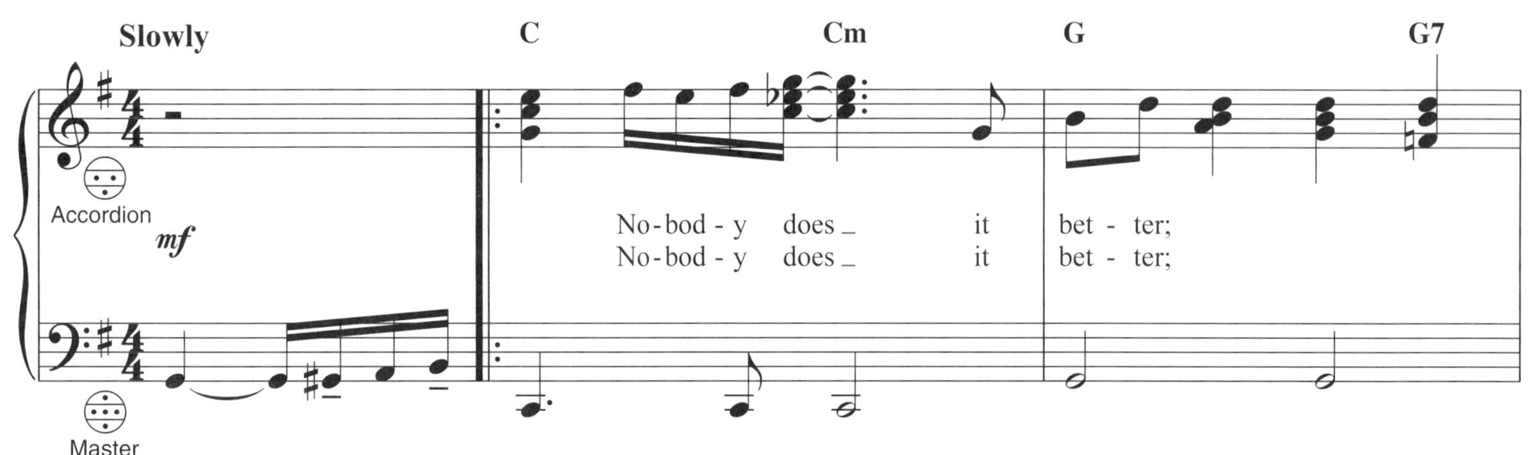

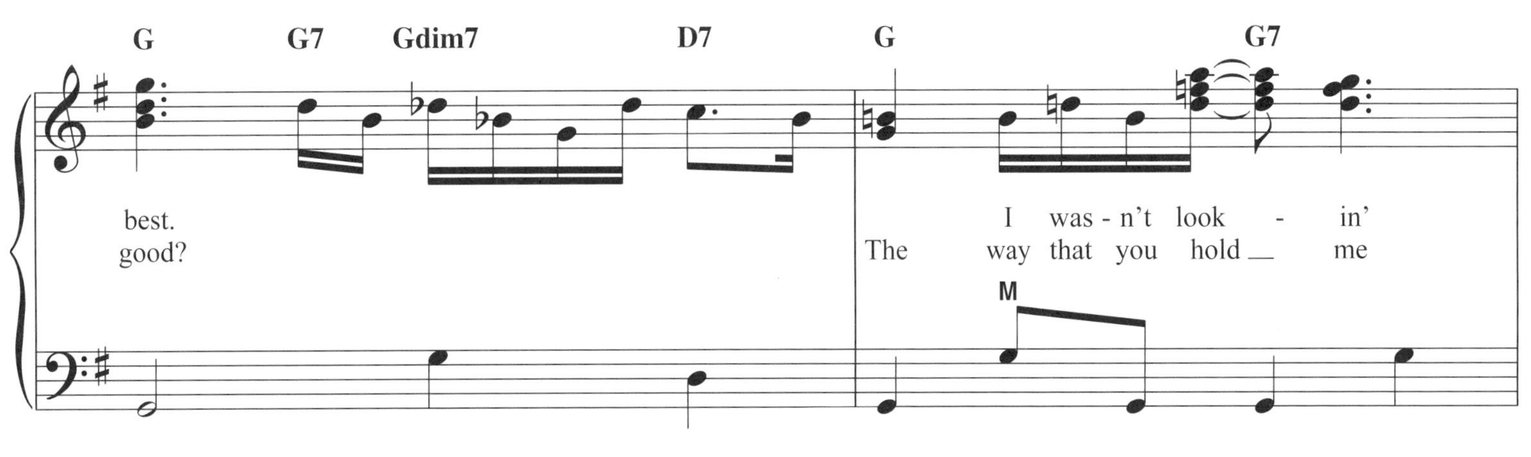
G G7 Gdim7 D7 G G7
best.
good?
I was - n't look - in'
The way that you hold _ me
M

C Cm G A9 A♭9
but some-how you found _ me.
when-ev - er you hold _ me,
I tried to hide _ from your love light,
there's some kind of mag - ic in - side you
M m M

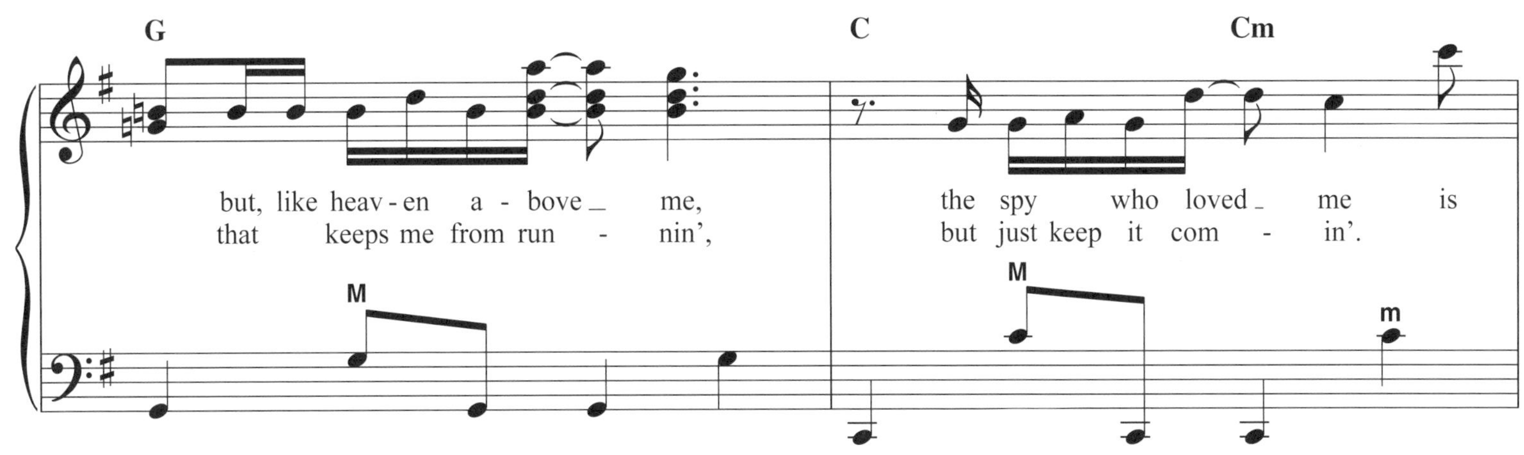
G C Cm
but, like heav - en a - bove _ me,
that keeps me from run - nin',
the spy who loved _ me is
but just keep it com - in'.
M M m

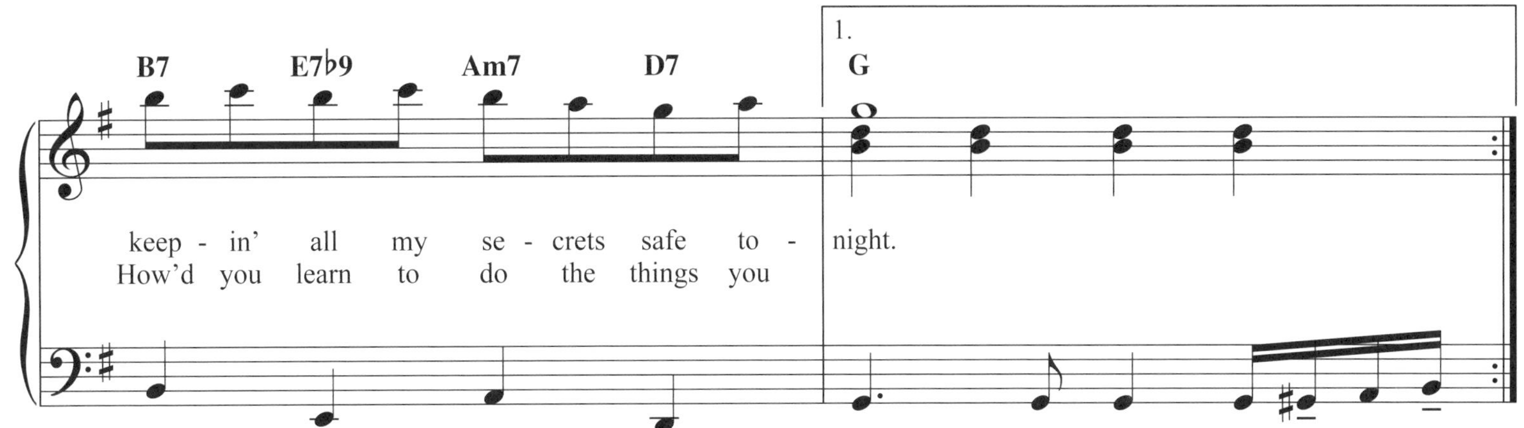
B7 E7♭9 Am7 D7
1.
G
keep - in' all my se - crets safe to - night.
How'd you learn to do the things you

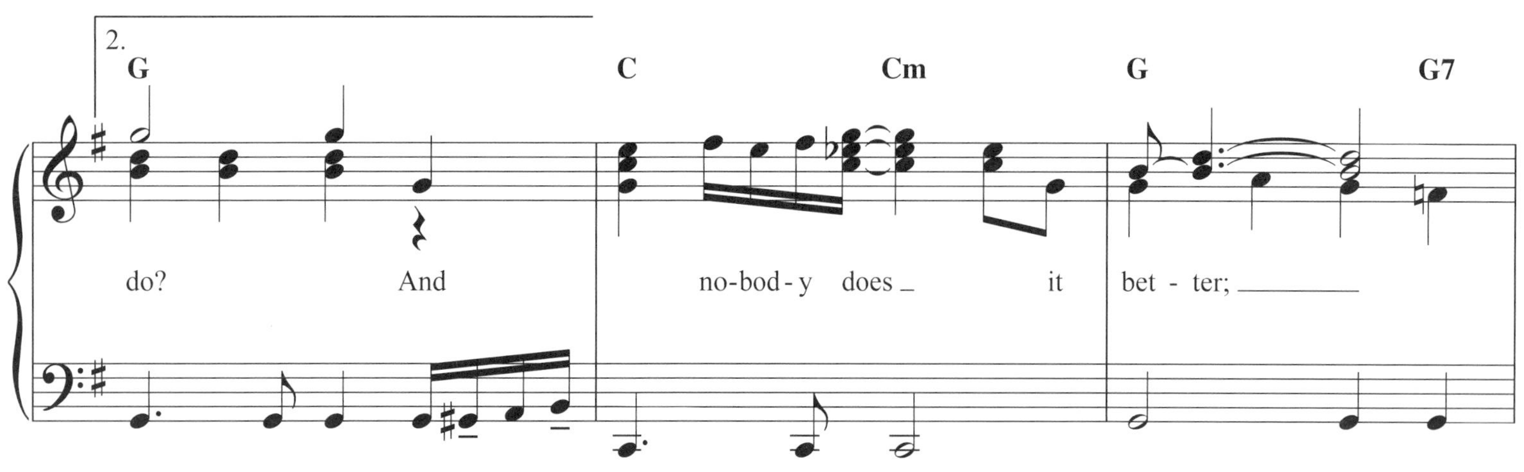
2.
G
C
Cm
G
G7
do? And
no-bod-y does it
bet - ter;

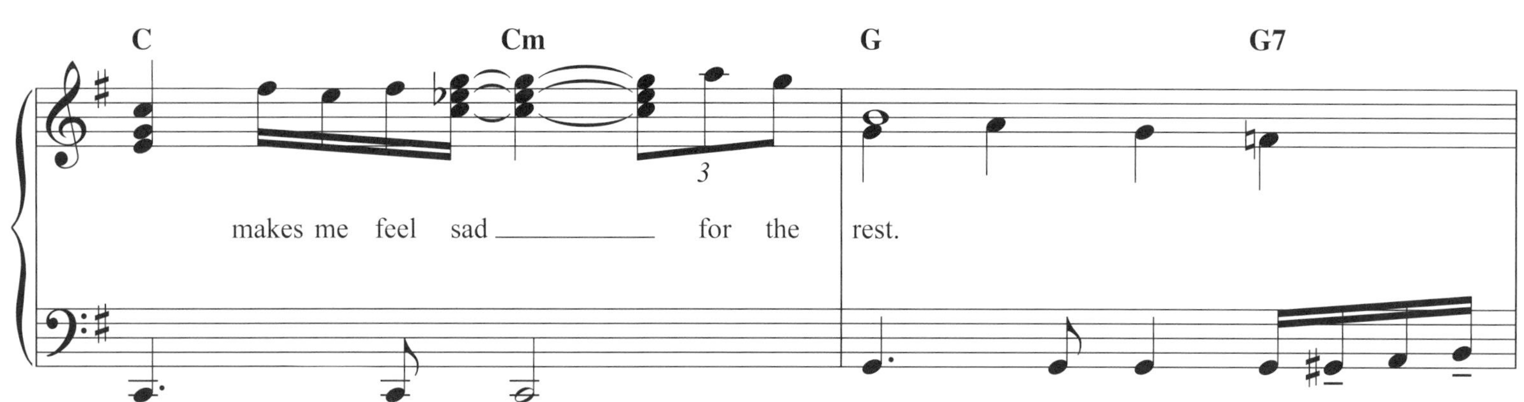
C
Cm
G
G7
3
makes me feel sad for the
rest.

C
Cm
B7♭9
Em7
Am7
G
No-bod-y does it
half as good as you.
Ba - by, ba - by,
m
M

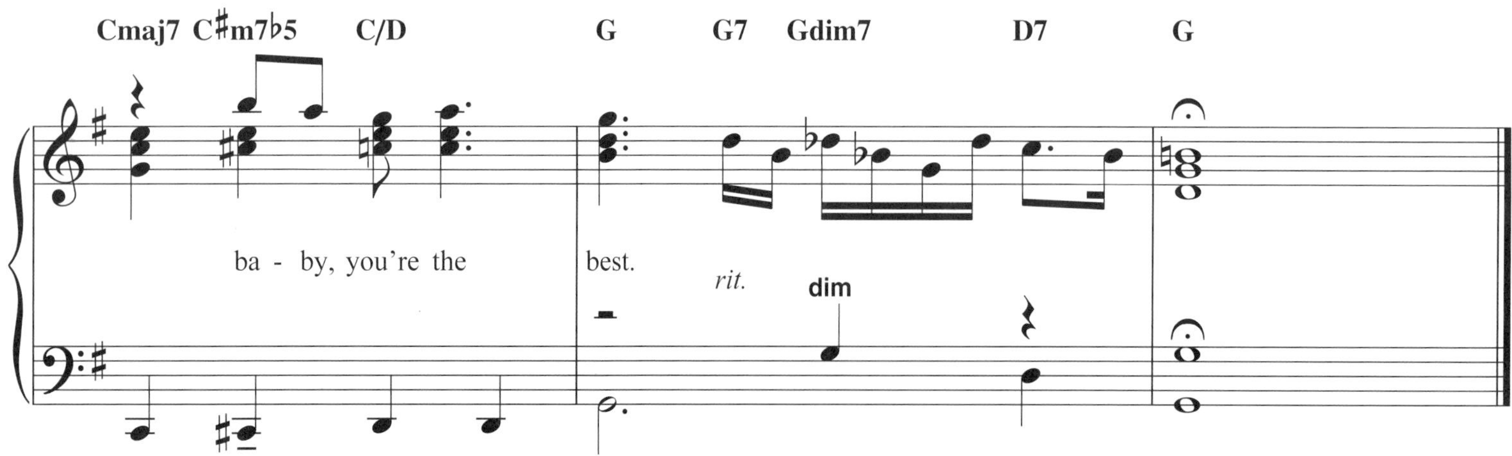
Cmaj7
C♯m7♭5
C/D
G
G7
Gdim7
D7
G
ba - by, you're the
best.
rit.
dim

(I've Had)

THE TIME OF MY LIFE

from DIRTY DANCING

Words and Music by FRANKE PREVITE,
JOHN DeNICOLA and DONALD MARKOWITZ

Dm
3
E♭
had the time of my life, and I owe it all to you.
m
M

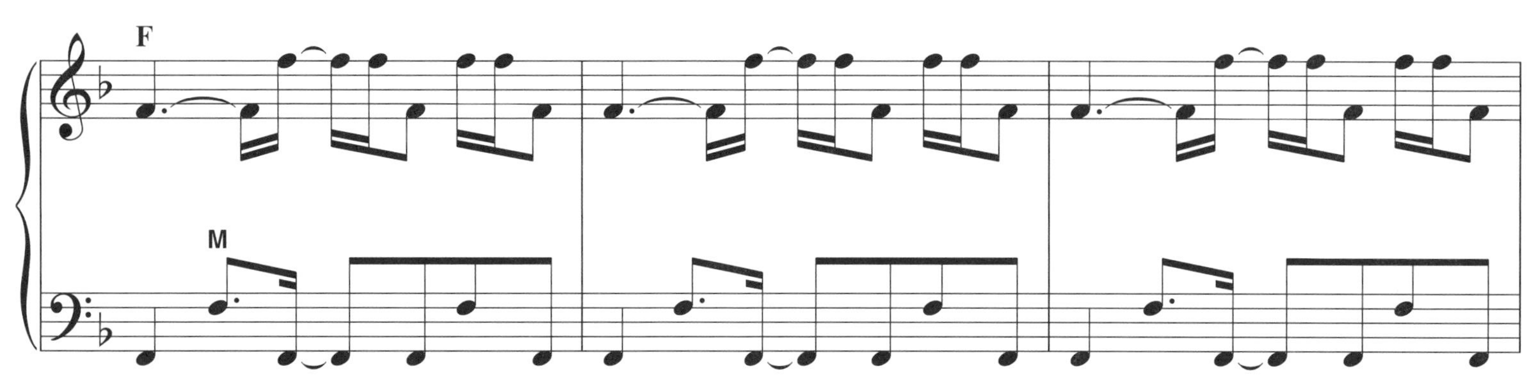
F
M

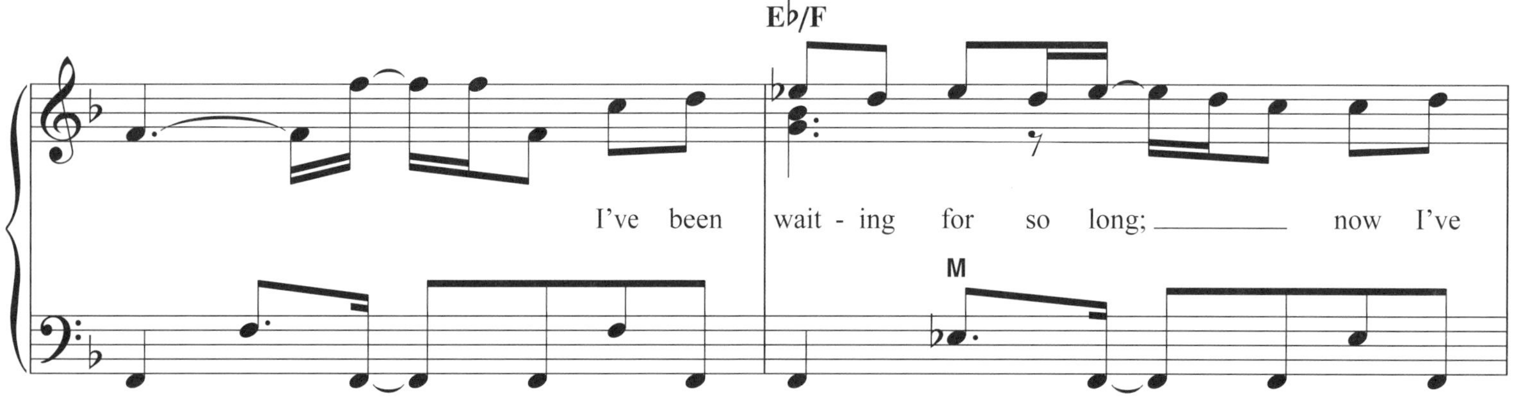
E♭/F
I've been wait - ing for so long; now I've
M

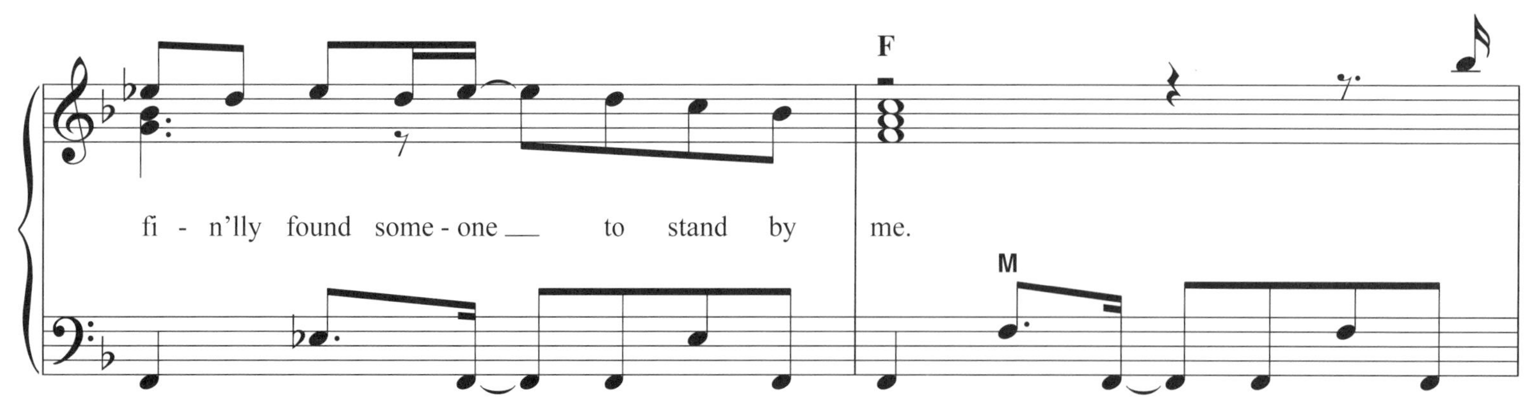
F
fi - n'lly found some - one to stand by me.
M

E♭/F
We saw the writ - ing on the wall as we
M

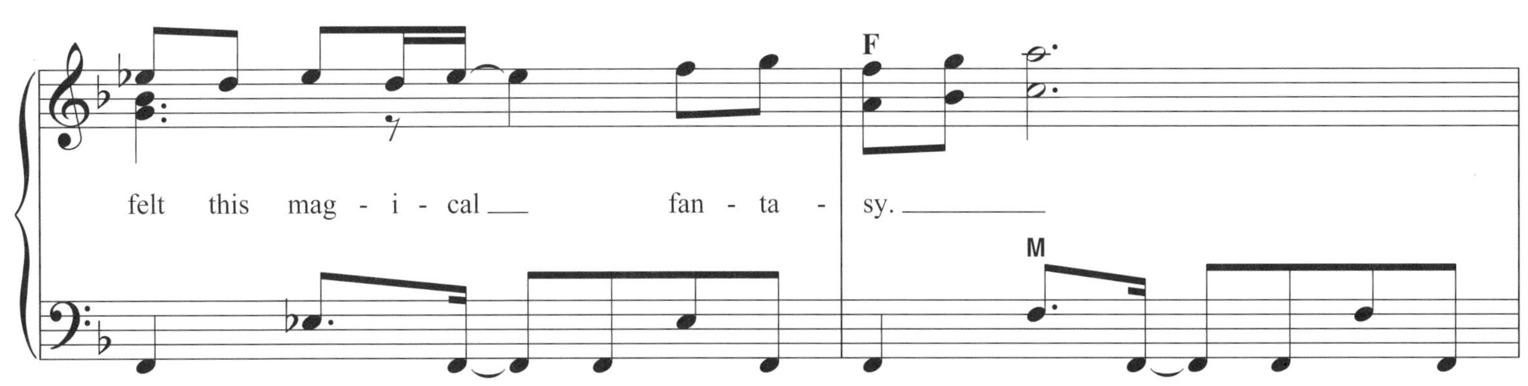
F
felt this mag - i - cal fan - ta - sy.
M

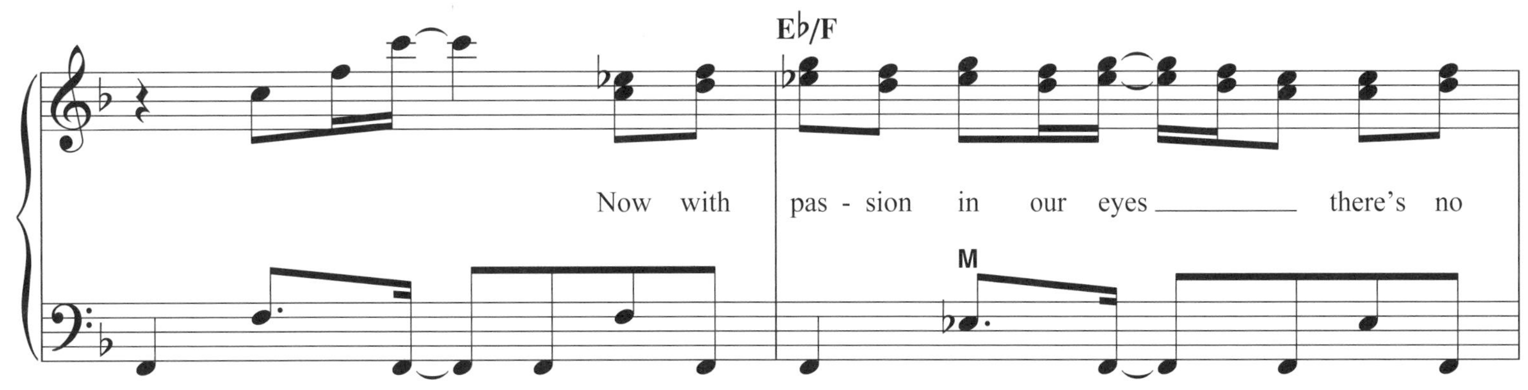
E♭/F
Now with pas - sion in our eyes there's no
M

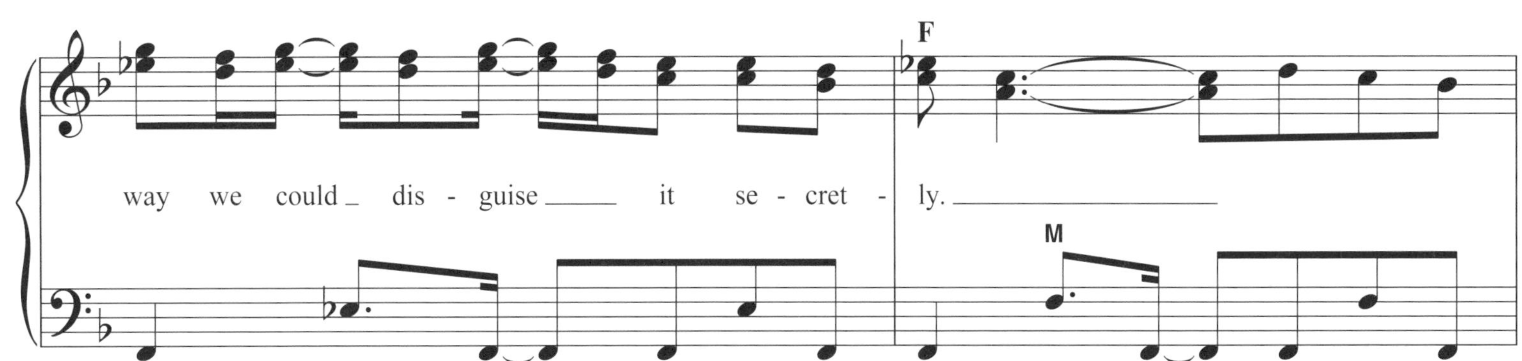
F
way we could dis - guise it se - cret - ly.
M

E♭/F
So we take each oth - er's hand 'cause we
M
M

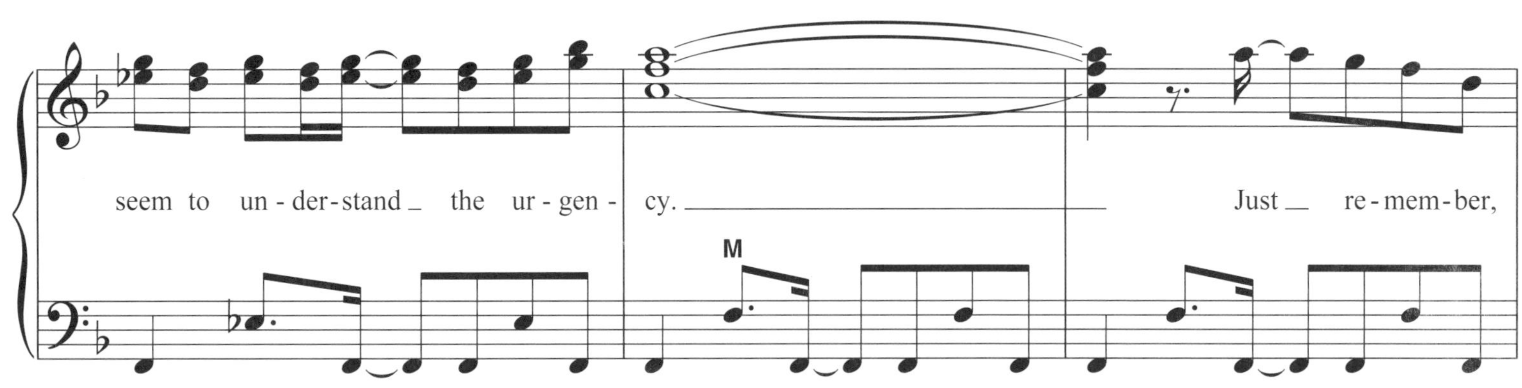
seem to un - der - stand the ur - gen - cy.
Just re - mem - ber,
M

A♭
you're the one thing I can't get e - nough
M
M

B♭
of.
So I'll tell you some - thing:
M

Csus
3
C
F
this could be love. Be - cause I've had
M
M

Dm
E♭
the time of my life. No, I nev - er felt this way be -
m
M

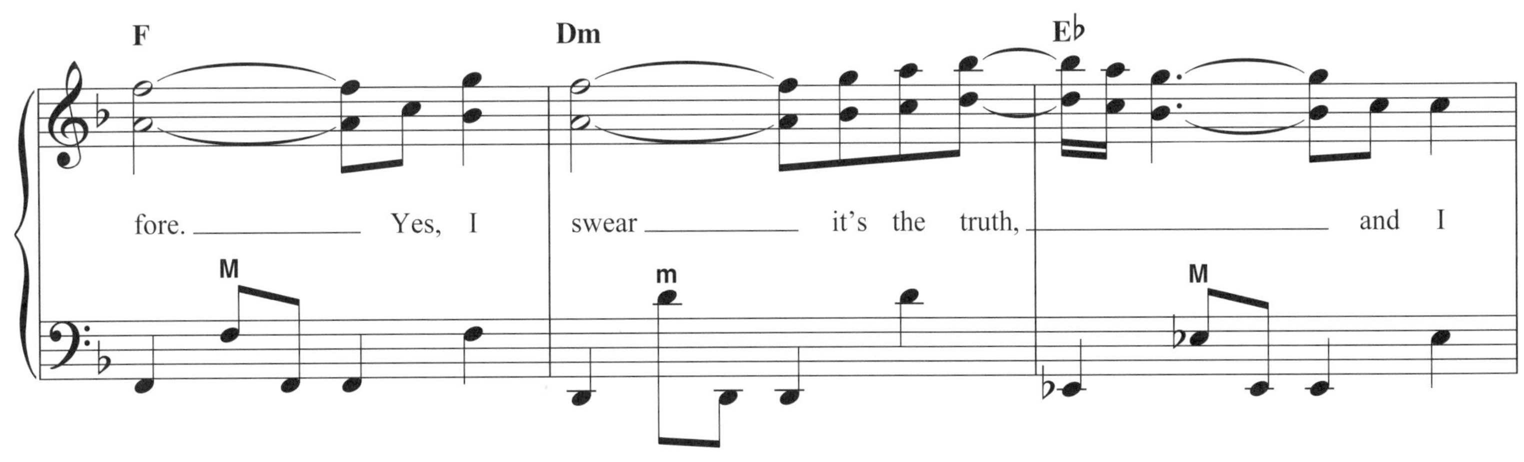
F
Dm
E♭
fore. Yes, I swear it's the truth, and I
M
m
M

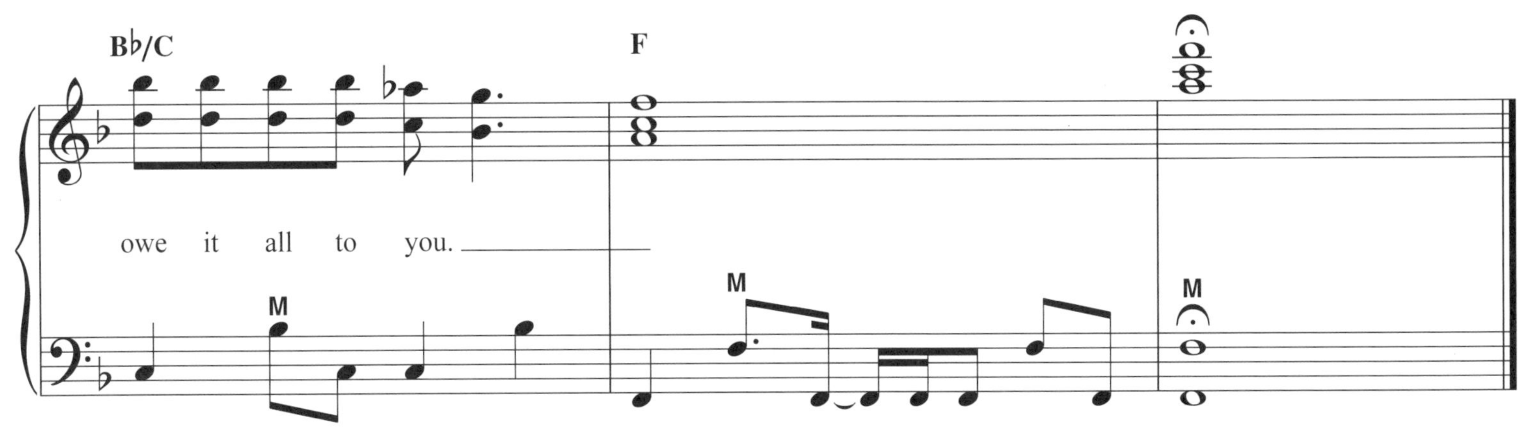
B♭/C
F
owe it all to you.
M
M
M

OVER THE RAINBOW
from THE WIZARD OF OZ

Music by HAROLD ARLEN
Lyric by E.Y. "YIP" HARBURG

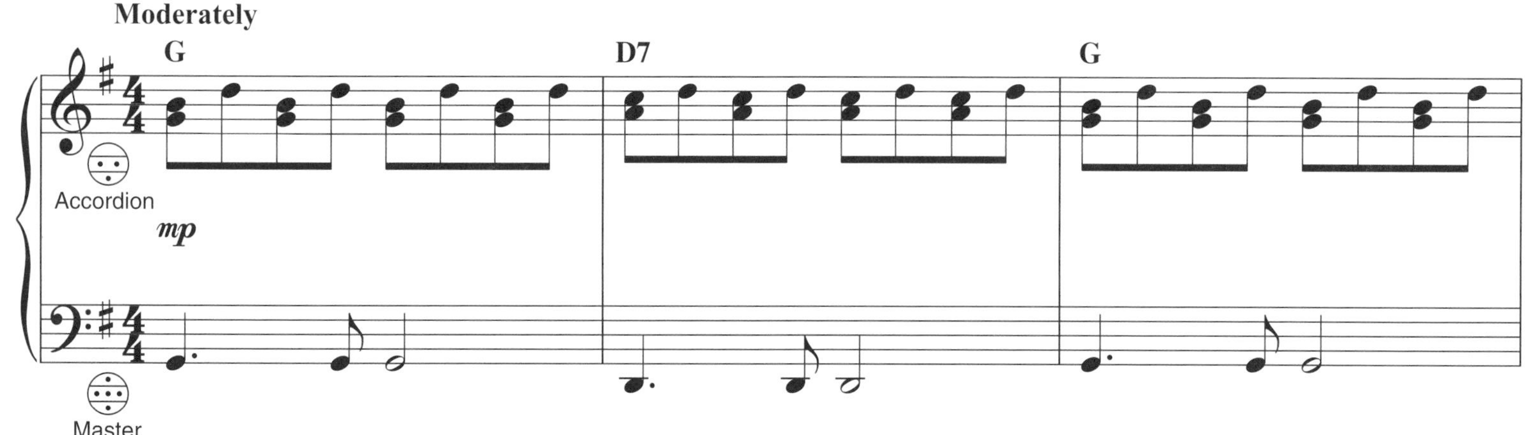

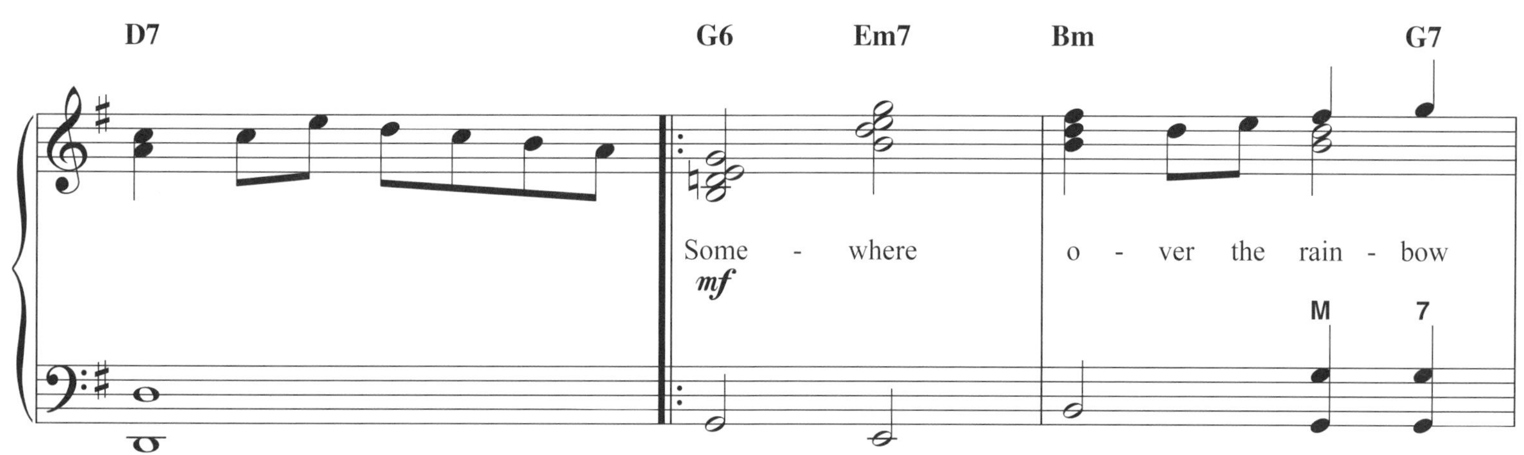

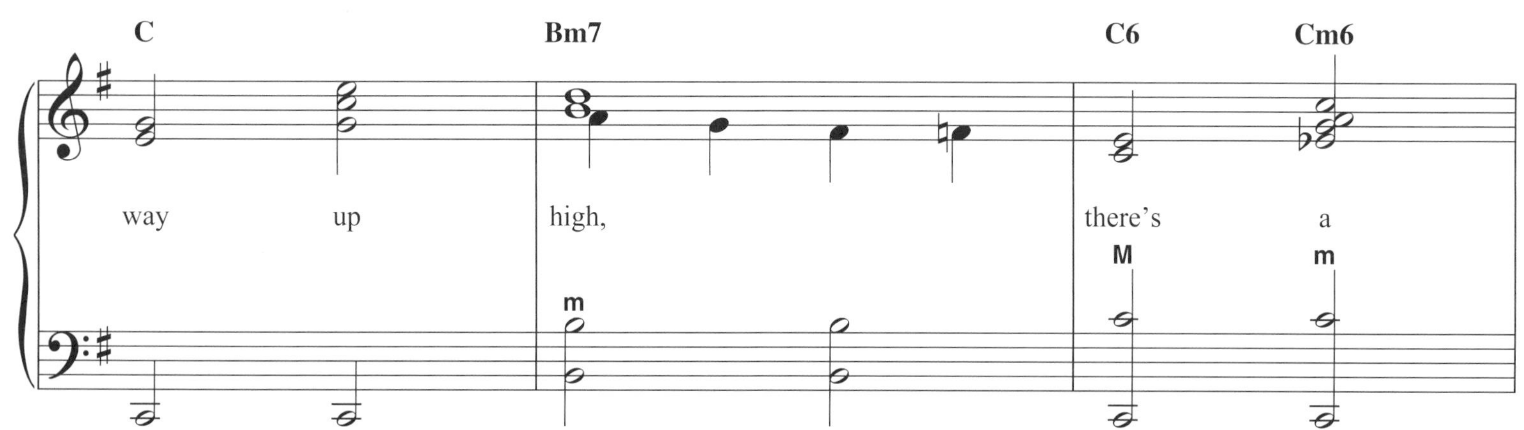

G
E7♭9
A7
Am/D
D7
G
Am/D
D7
land that I heard of once in a lull - a - by.

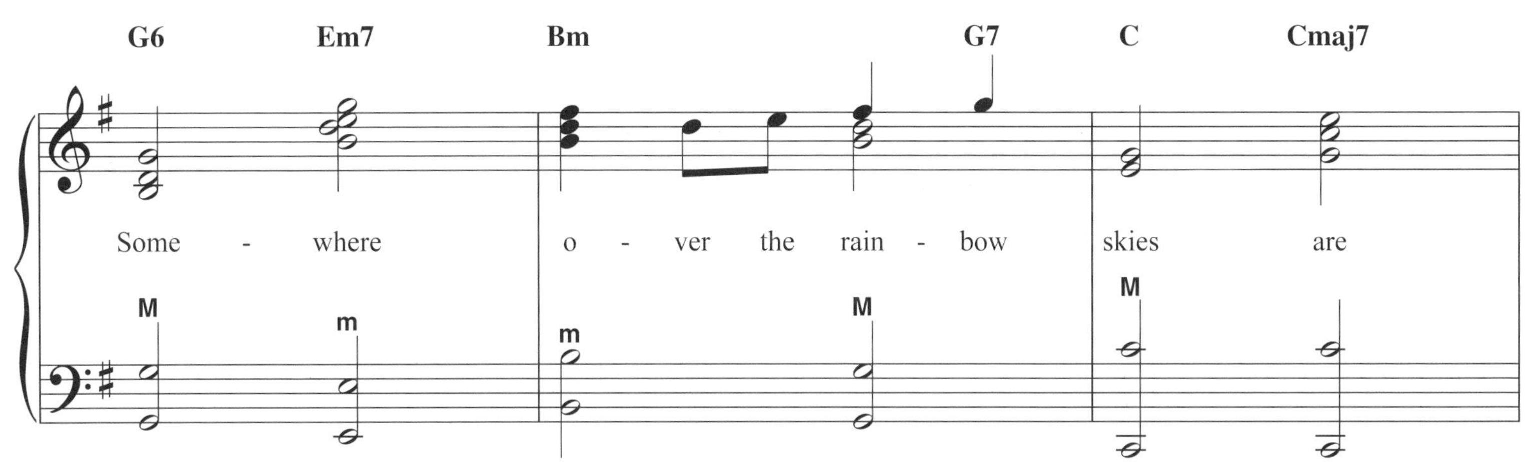
G6
Em7
Bm
G7
C
Cmaj7
Some - where o - ver the rain - bow skies are
M
m
m
M
M

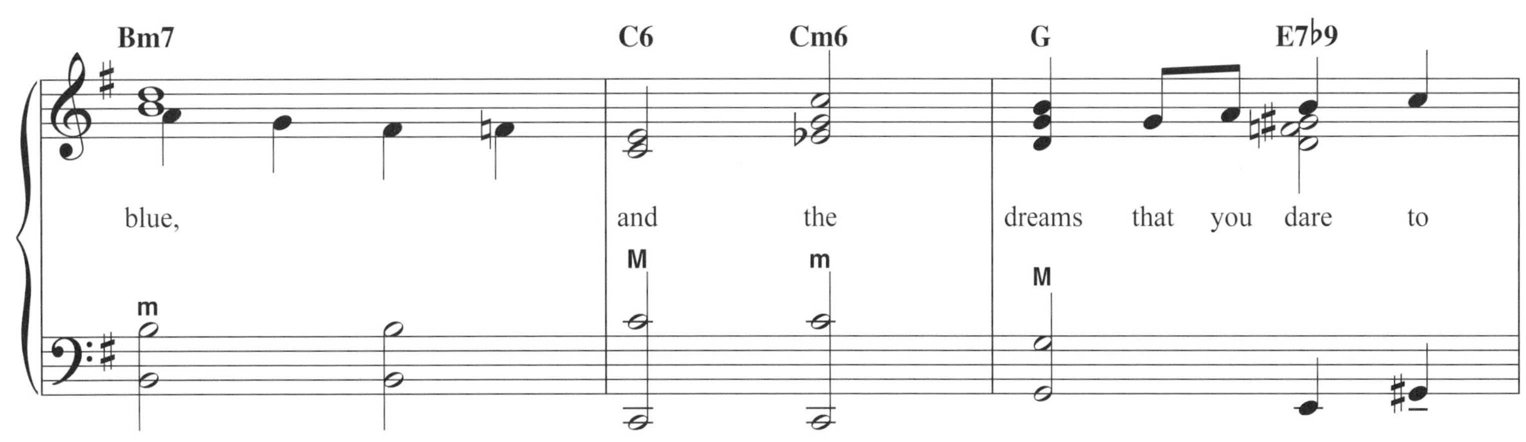
Bm7
C6
Cm6
G
E7♭9
blue, and the dreams that you dare to
m
M
m
M

A7
D7
G
dream real - ly do come true. Some - day I'll wish up - on a star and
mp
7
7

D7
G6
Am
D7
wake up where the clouds are far be - hind me. Where
m
7

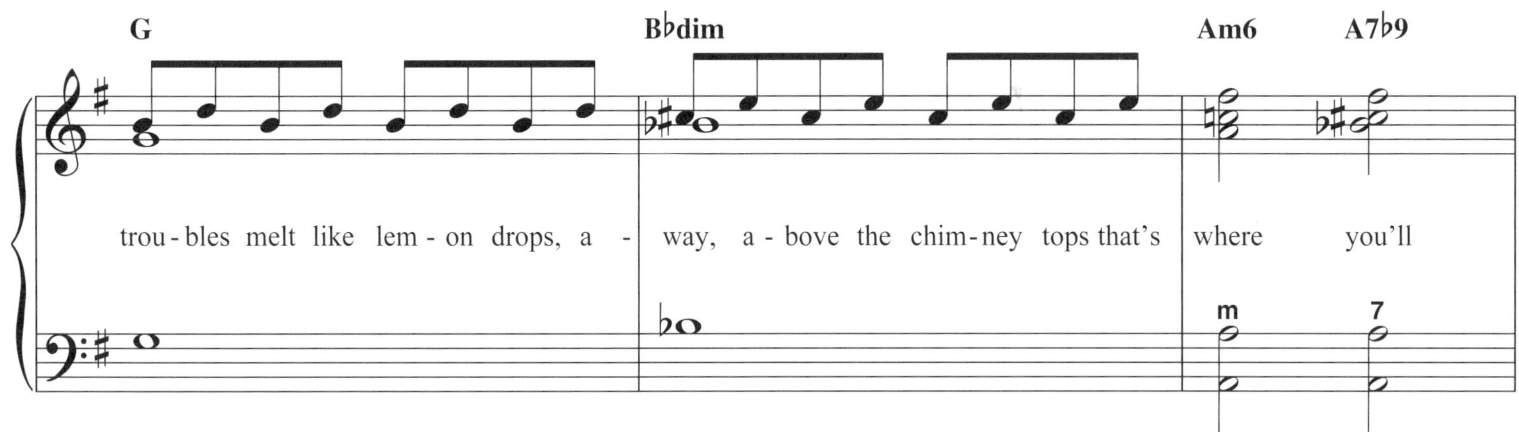
G
B♭dim
Am6
A7♭9
trou - bles melt like lem - on drops, a - way, a - bove the chim - ney tops that's where you'll
m
7

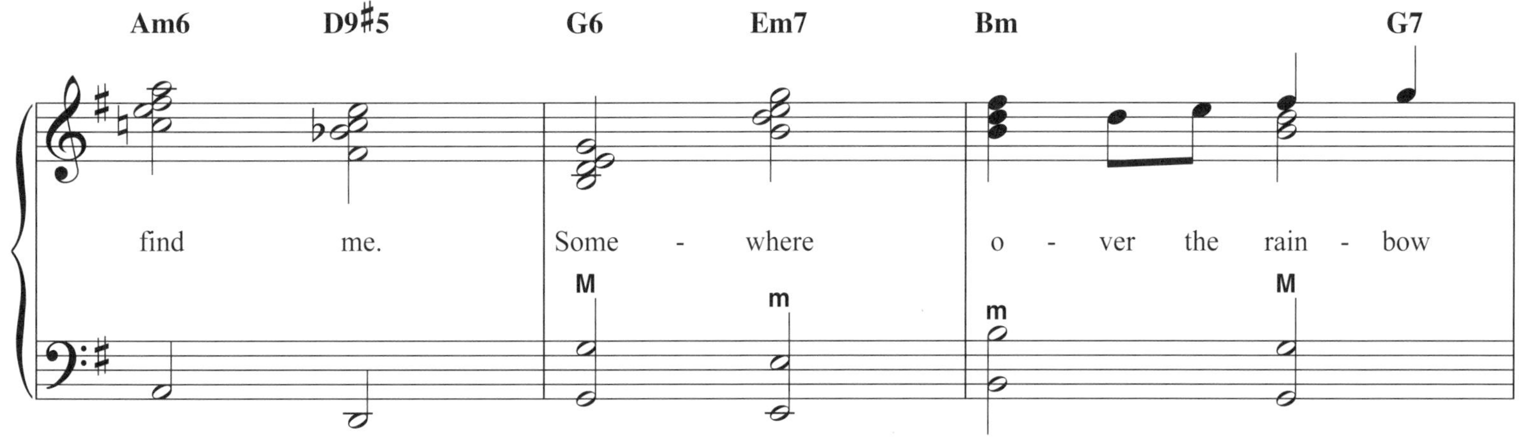
Am6
D9♯5
G6
Em7
Bm
G7
find me. Some - where o - ver the rain - bow
M
m
m
M

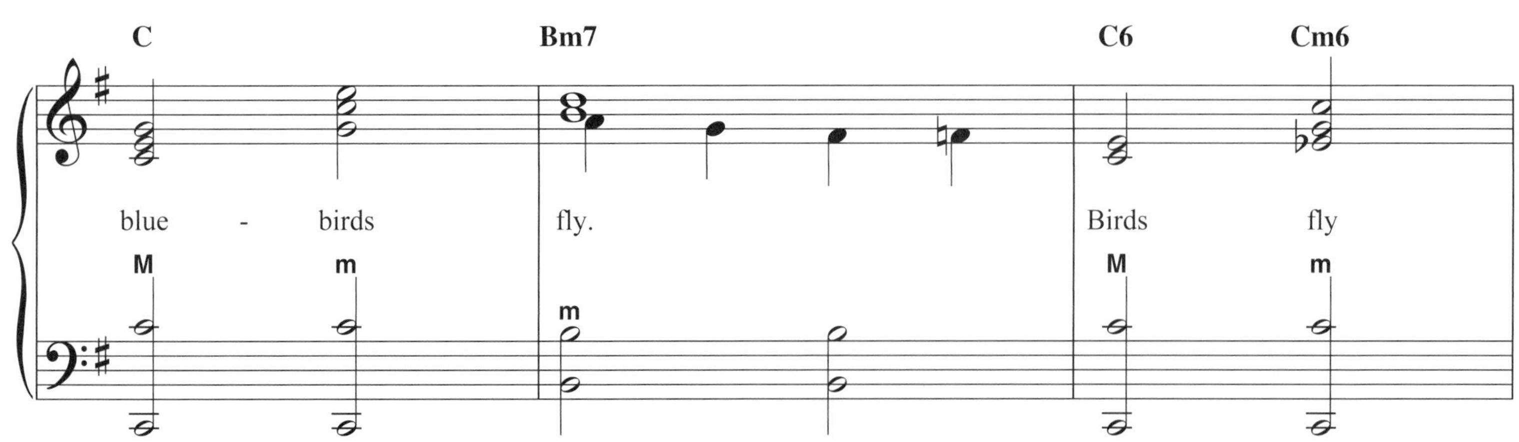
C
Bm7
C6
Cm6
blue - birds fly. Birds fly
M
m
m
M
m

1.
G
E7♭9
A7
Am/D
D7
G
D9
D7♭9
o - ver the rain - bow, why then, oh why can't I?
M
7
7
7
M
7
2.
G6
G
Am
I?
M
m
G
Am7
D7
G
If hap - py lit - tle blue - birds fly be -
M
m
M
Am
D7
G6
yond the rain - bow, why oh why can't I?
rit.
pp
m
M

SHALLOW
from A STAR IS BORN

Words and Music by STEFANI GERMANOTTA,
MARK RONSON, ANDREW WYATT
and ANTHONY ROSSOMANDO

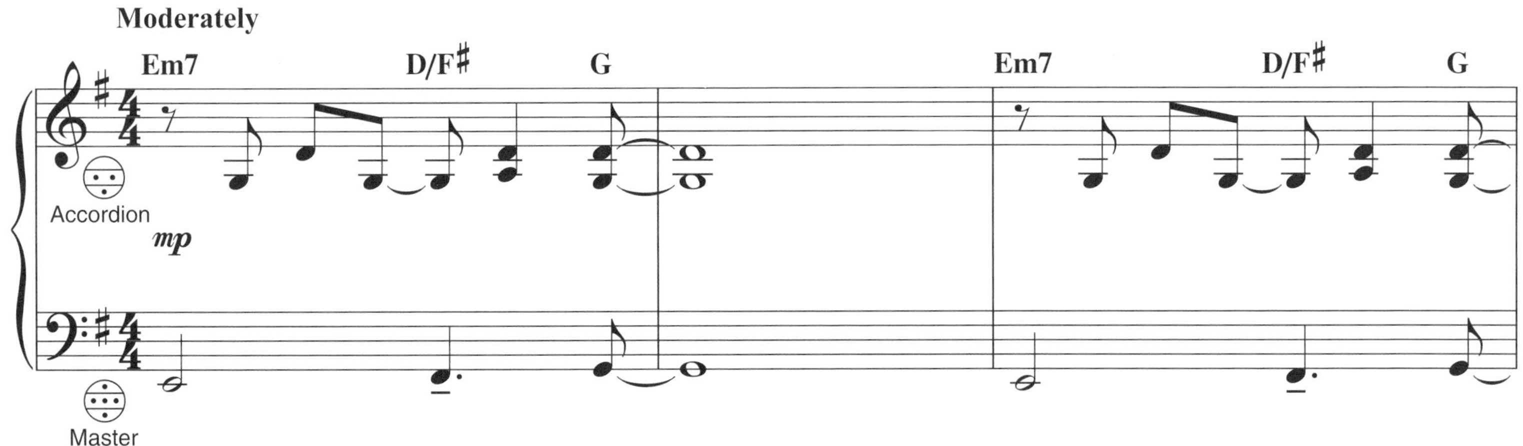

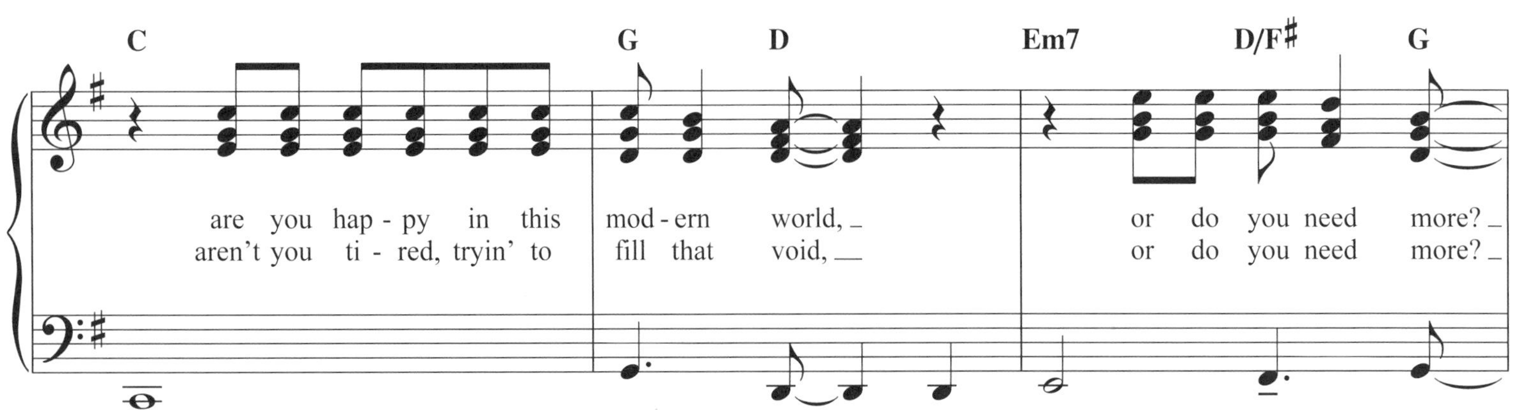

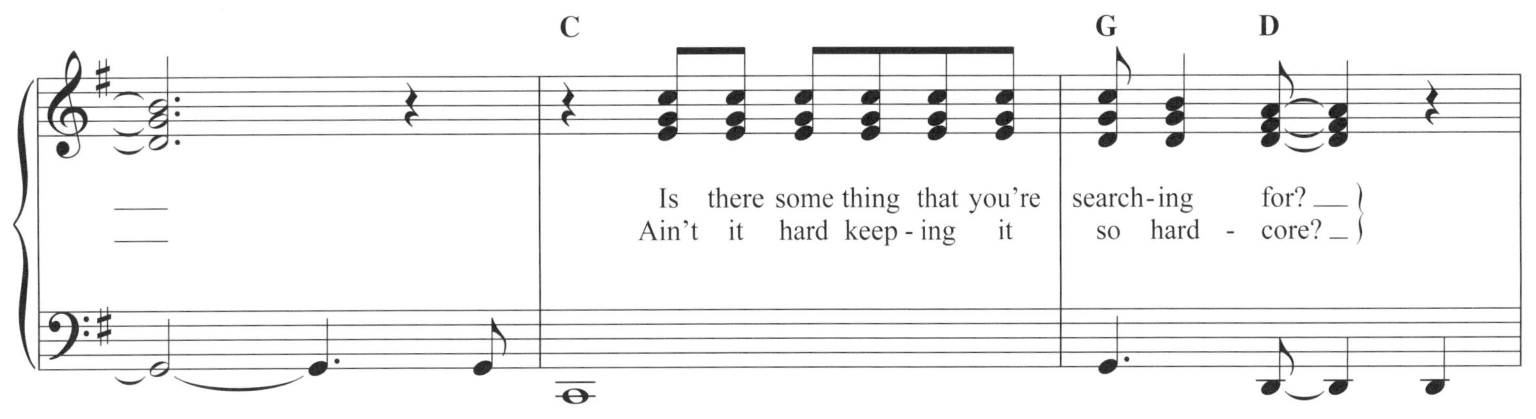
C
G
D
Is there some thing that you're search-ing for?
Ain't it hard keep-ing it so hard - core?

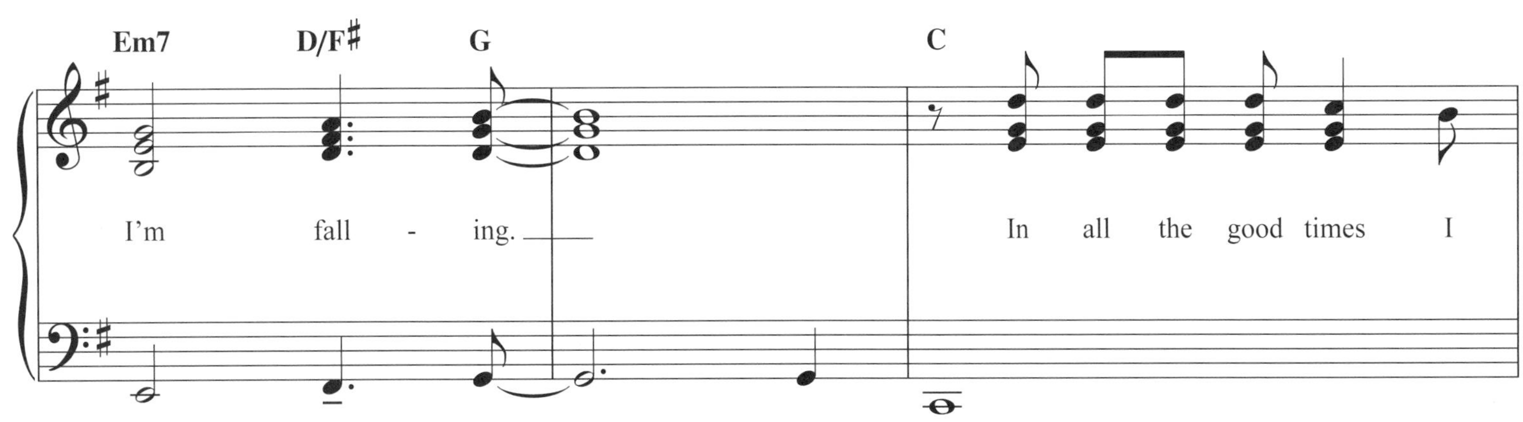
Em7
D/F♯
G
C
I'm fall - ing.
In all the good times I

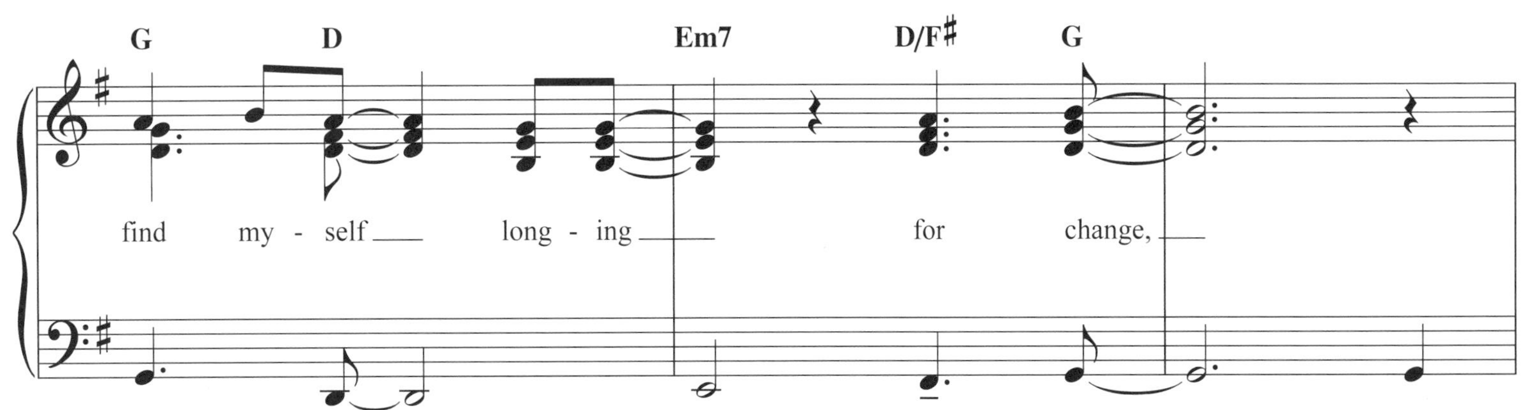
G
D
Em7
D/F♯
G
find my - self long - ing for change,

C
G
D
Am
Am/G
and in the bad times I fear my - self.
I'm off the deep end.

D/F♯
G
D
Em7
Watch as I dive in. I'll nev-er meet the ground.

Am
Am/G
D/F♯
G
D
Crash through the sur-face, where they can't hurt us. We're far from the shal-low now.

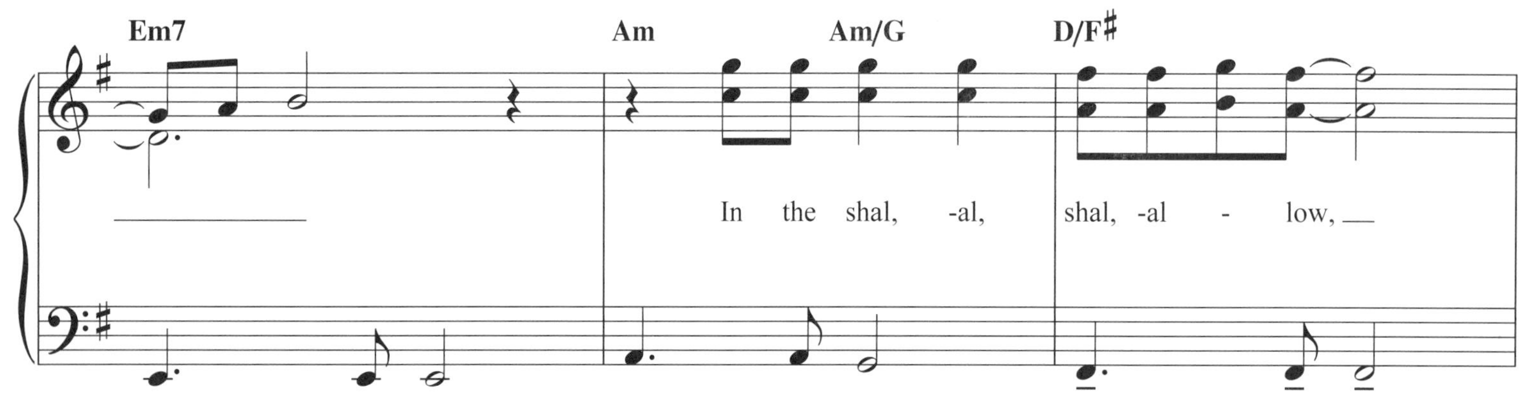
Em7
Am
Am/G
D/F♯
In the shal, -al, shal, -al-low,

G
D
Em7
Am
Am/G
in the shal, shal, -al, -al, -al-low.
In the shal, -al,

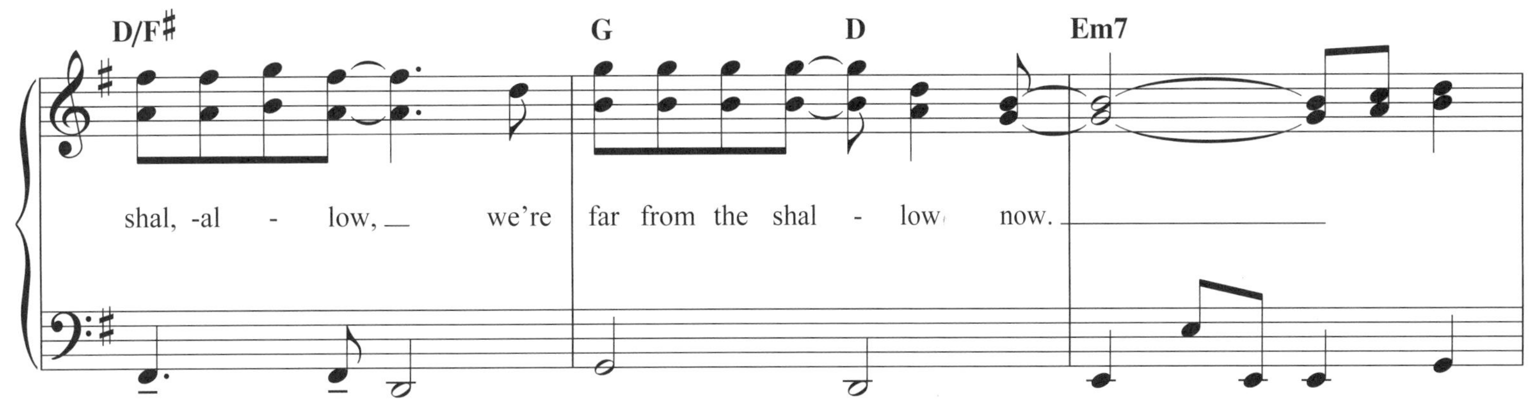
D/F♯
G
D
Em7
shal, -al - low, we're far from the shal - low now.

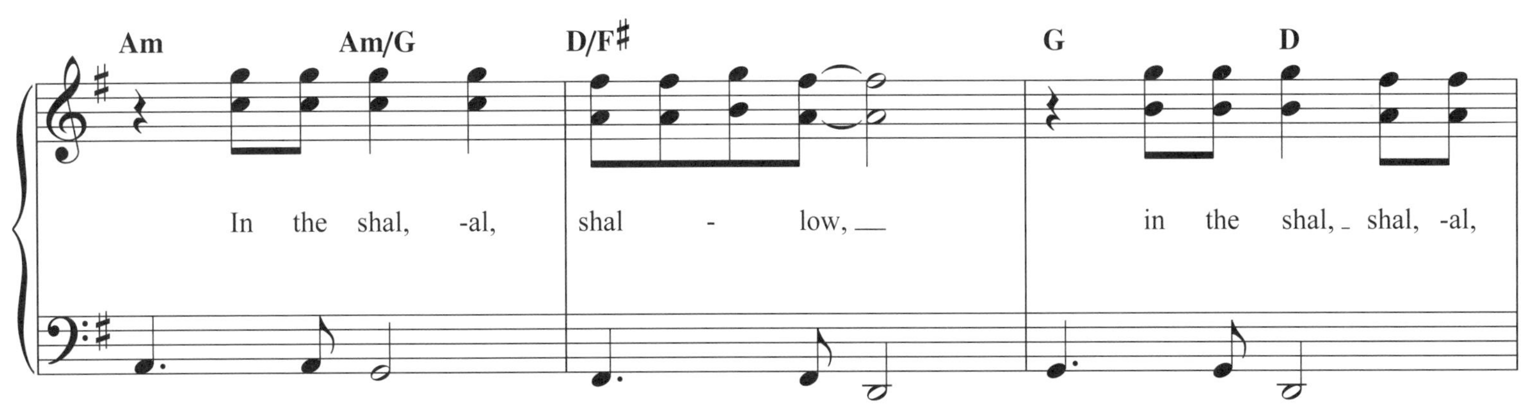
Am
Am/G
D/F♯
G
D
In the shal, -al, shal - low, in the shal, shal, -al,

Em7
Am
Am/G
D/F♯
-al, -al - low. In the shal, -al, shal - low, we're

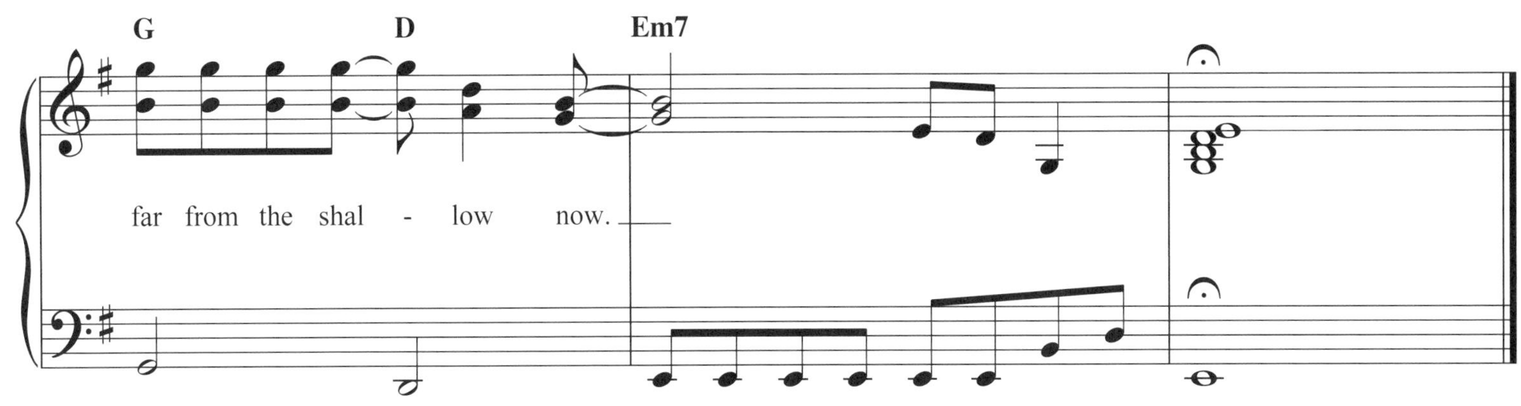
G
D
Em7
far from the shal - low now.

SINGIN' IN THE RAIN

from SINGIN' IN THE RAIN

Lyric by ARTHUR FREED
Music by NACIO HERB BROWN

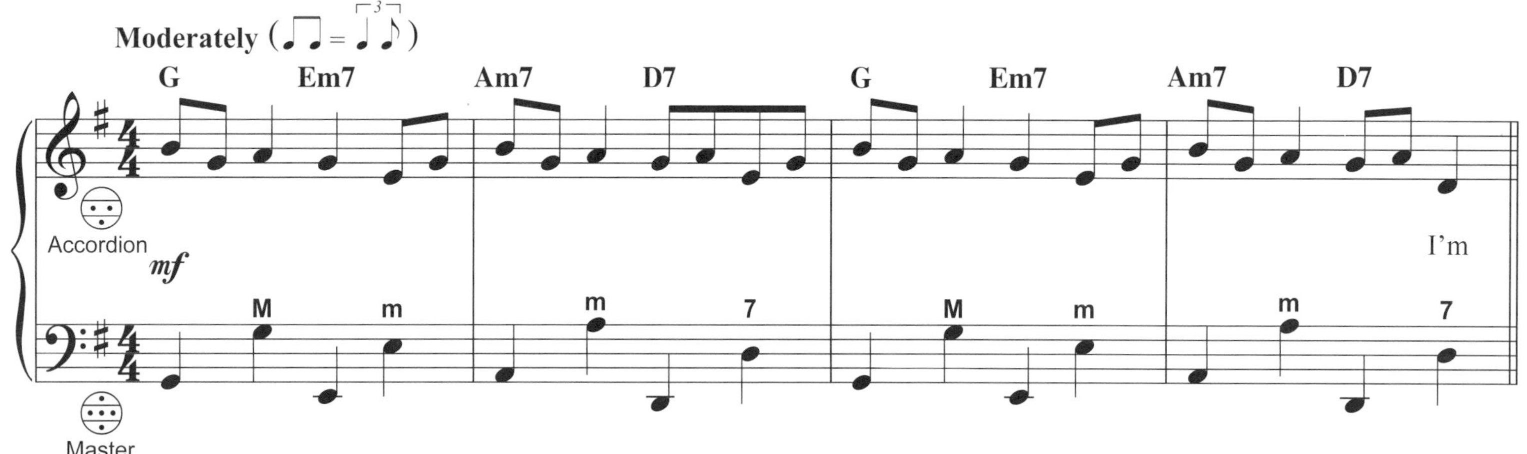

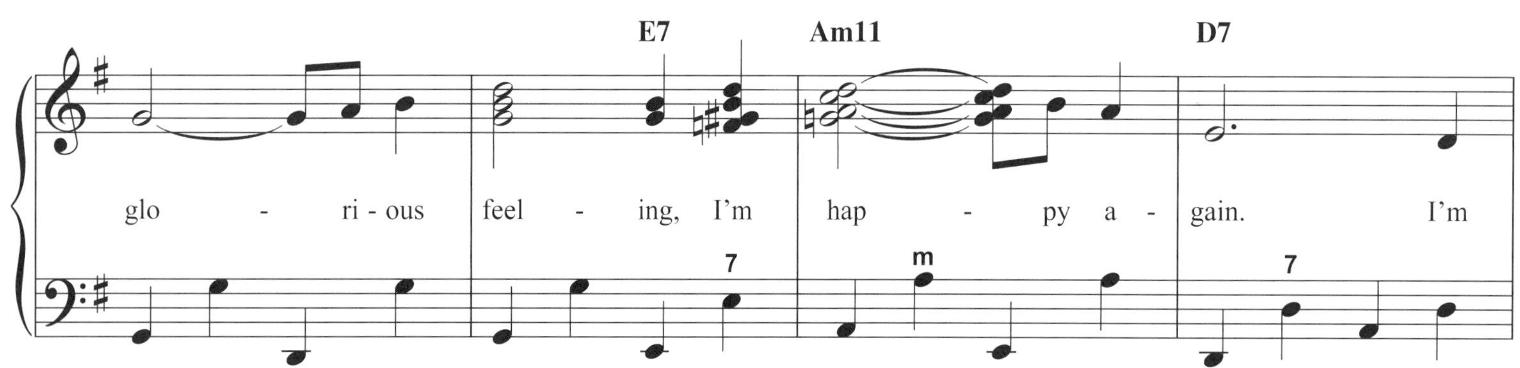

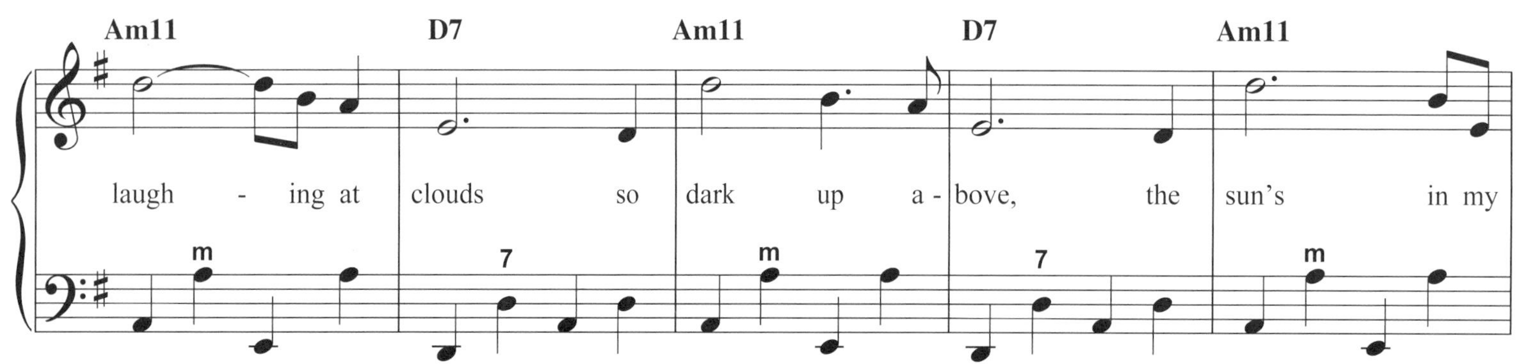

D7
G
heart and I'm read - y for love. Let the storm - y clouds chase ev-'ry-
7
M

E7
Am11
one ___ from the place. Come on ___ with the rain, I've a smile ___ on my
7
m

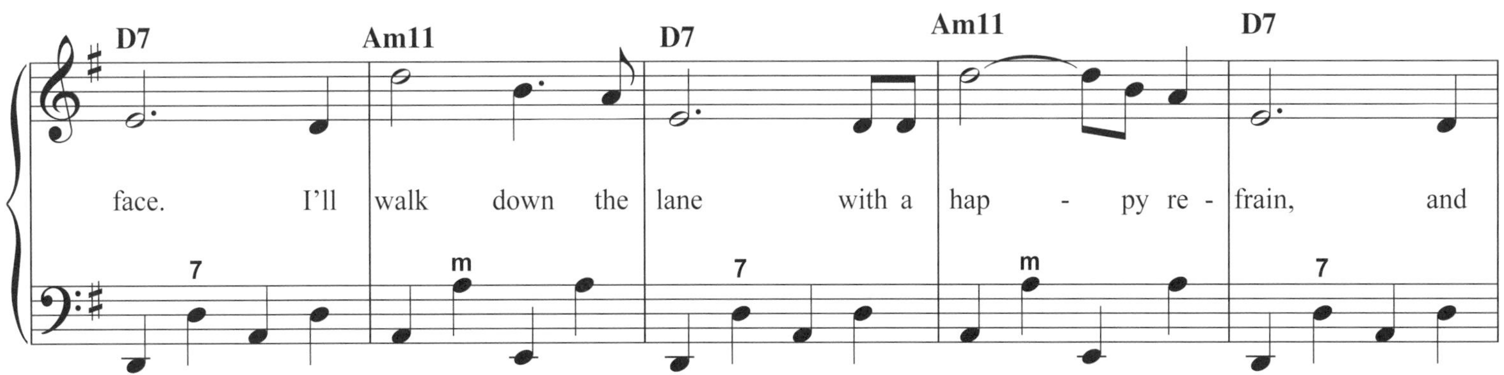
D7
Am11
D7
Am11
D7
face. I'll walk down the lane with a hap - py re - frain, and
7
m
7
m
7

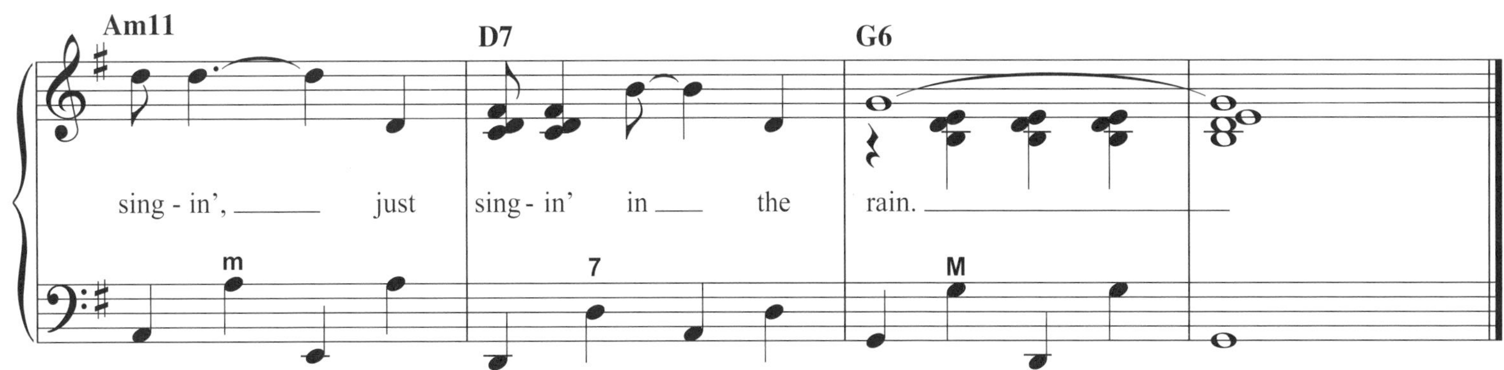
Am11
D7
G6
sing - in', ___ just sing - in' in ___ the rain. ___
m
7
M

A TIME FOR US

(Love Theme)

from the Paramount Picture ROMEO AND JULIET

Words by LARRY KUSIK and EDDIE SNYDER
Music by NINO ROTA

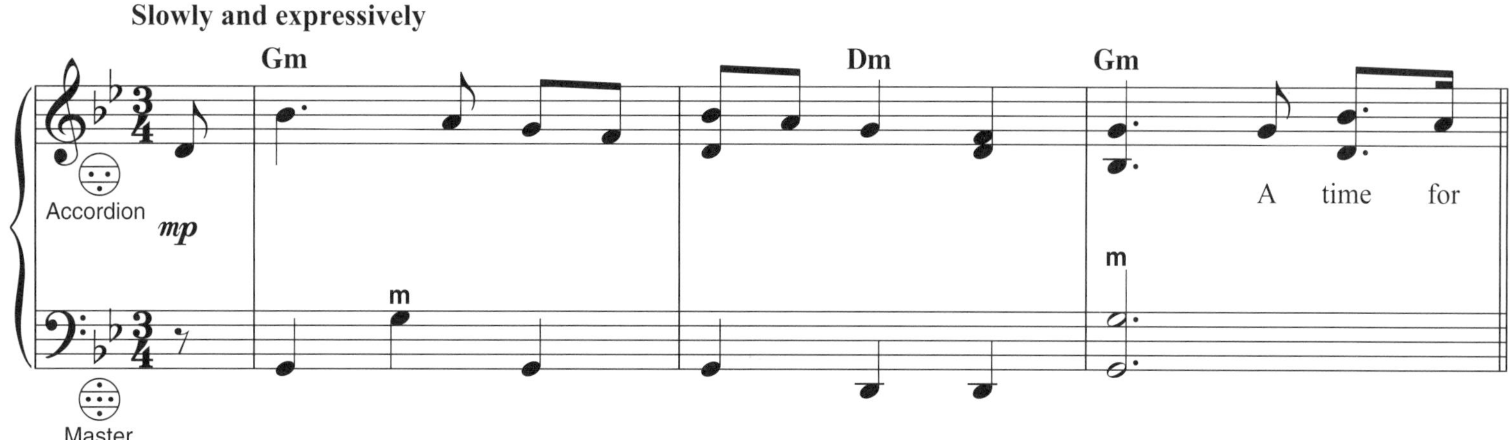

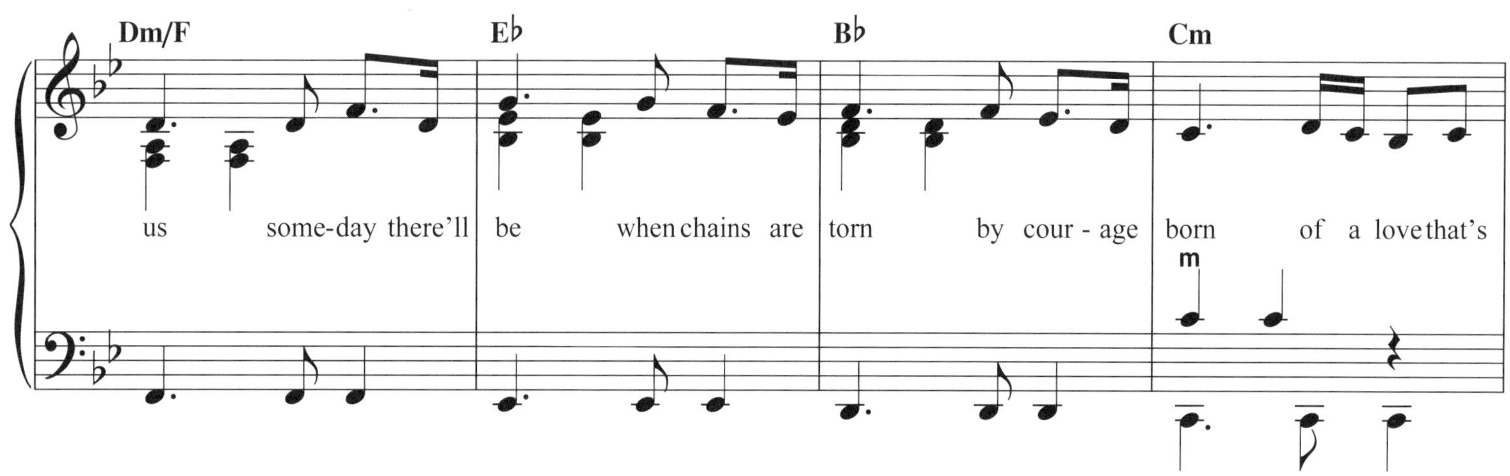

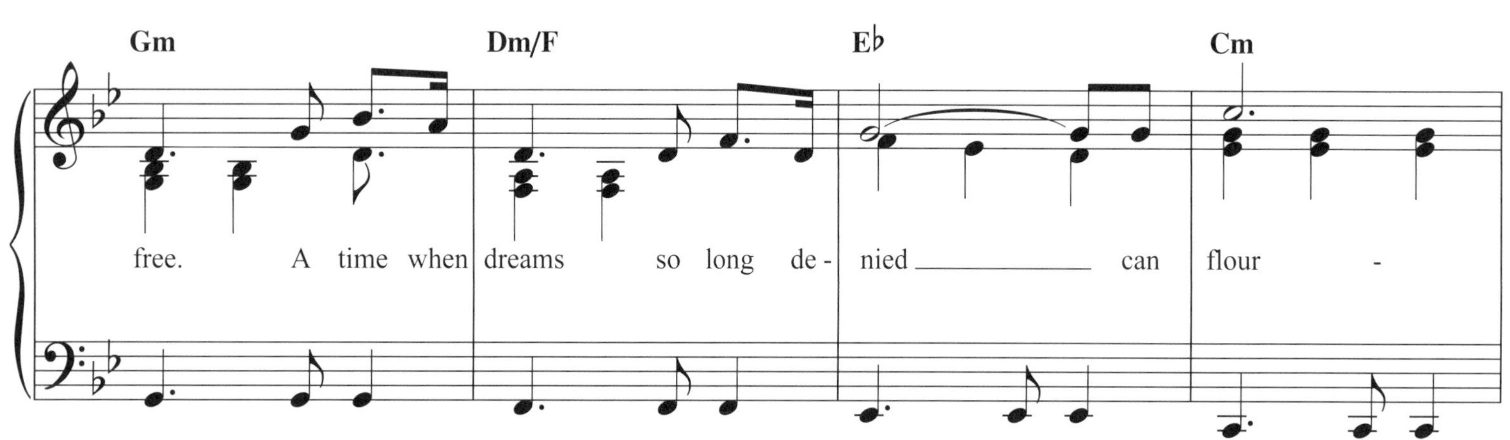

Dm
Gm
Dm
Gm
ish as we un - veil the love we now must hide. A
f
m
m
m

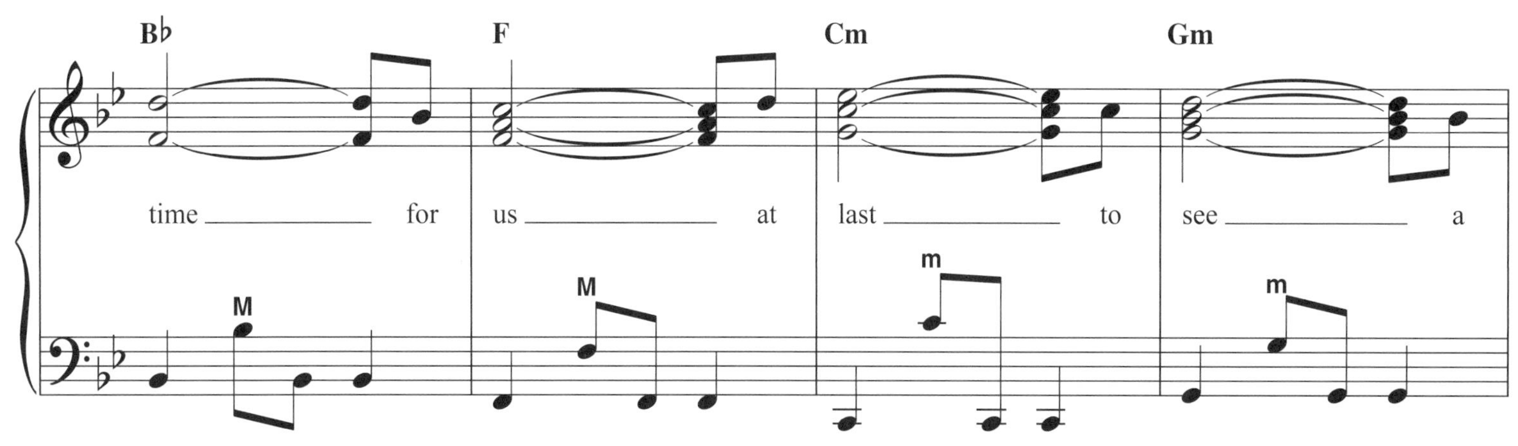
B♭
F
Cm
Gm
time for us at last to see a
M
M
m
m

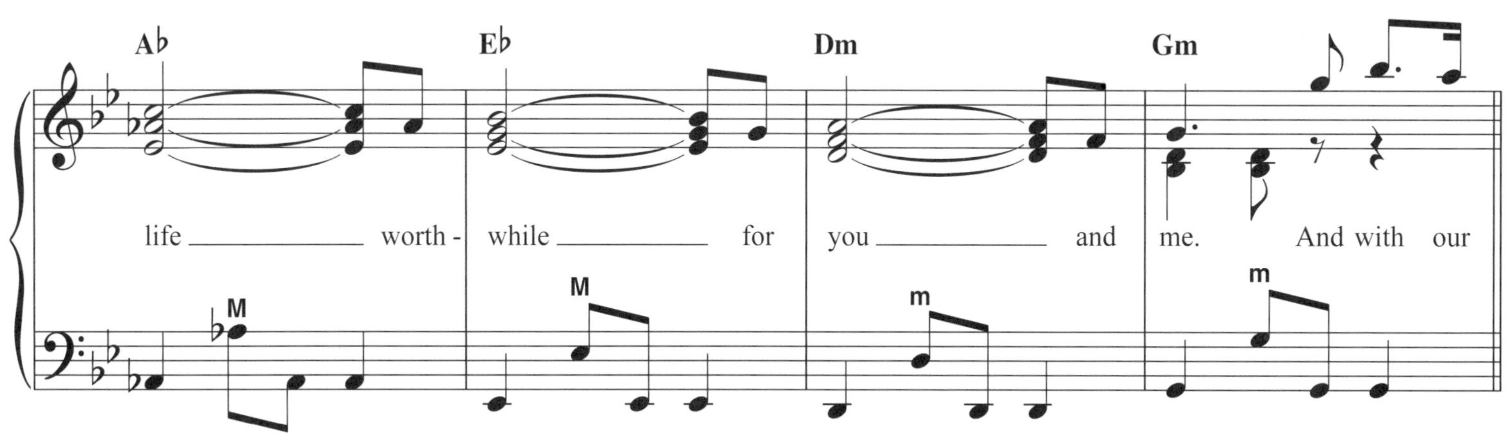
A♭
E♭
Dm
Gm
life worth - while for you and me. And with our
M
M
m
m

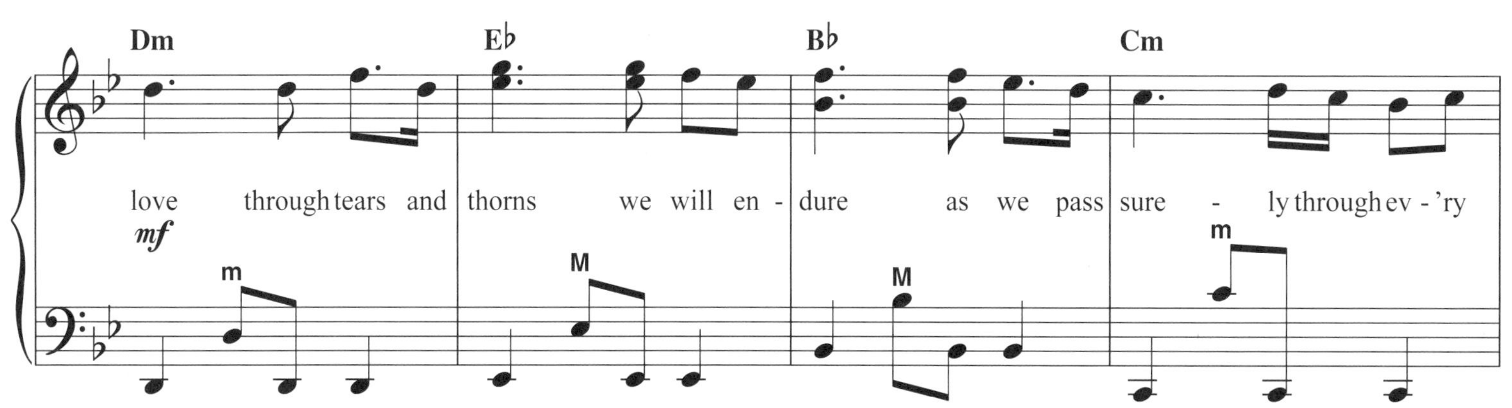
Dm
E♭
B♭
Cm
love through tears and thorns we will en - dure as we pass sure - ly through ev - 'ry
mf
m
M
M
m

Gm
Dm/F
E♭
Cm
storm. A time for us some-day there'll be ___ a new
m
M
m

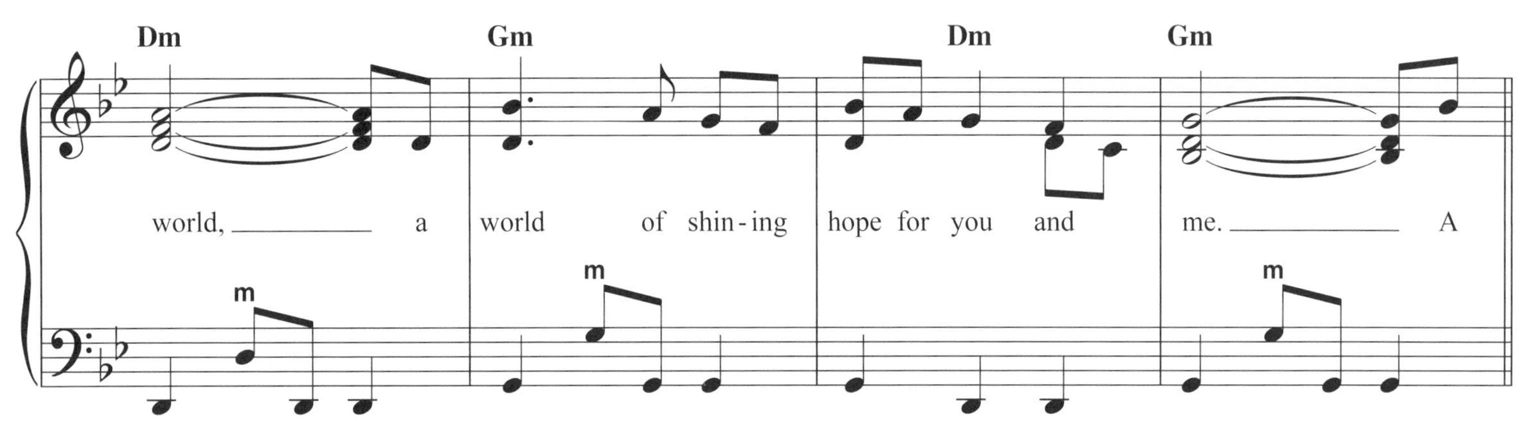

Dm
Gm
Dm
Gm
world, ___ a world of shin-ing hope for you and me. ___ A
m
m
m

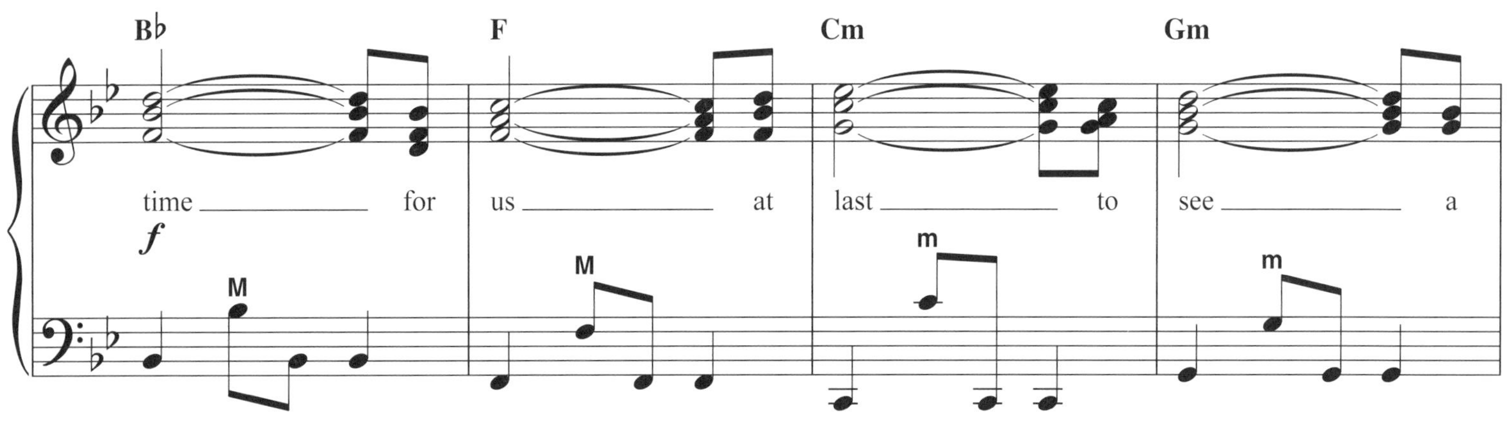

B♭
F
Cm
Gm
time ___ for us ___ at last ___ to see ___ a
f
M
M
m
m

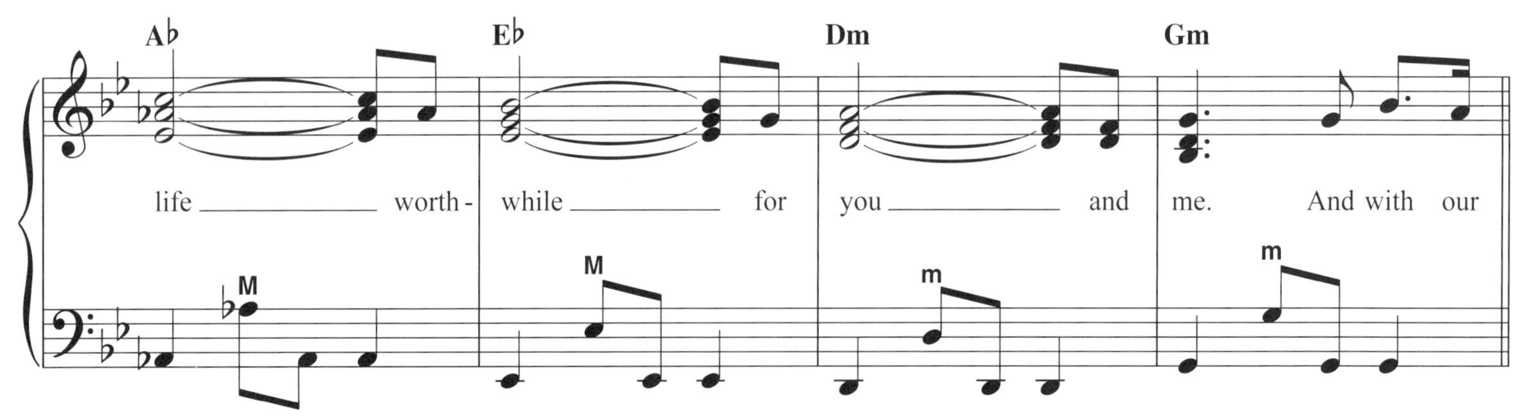

A♭
E♭
Dm
Gm
life ___ worth-while ___ for you ___ and me. And with our
M
M
m
m

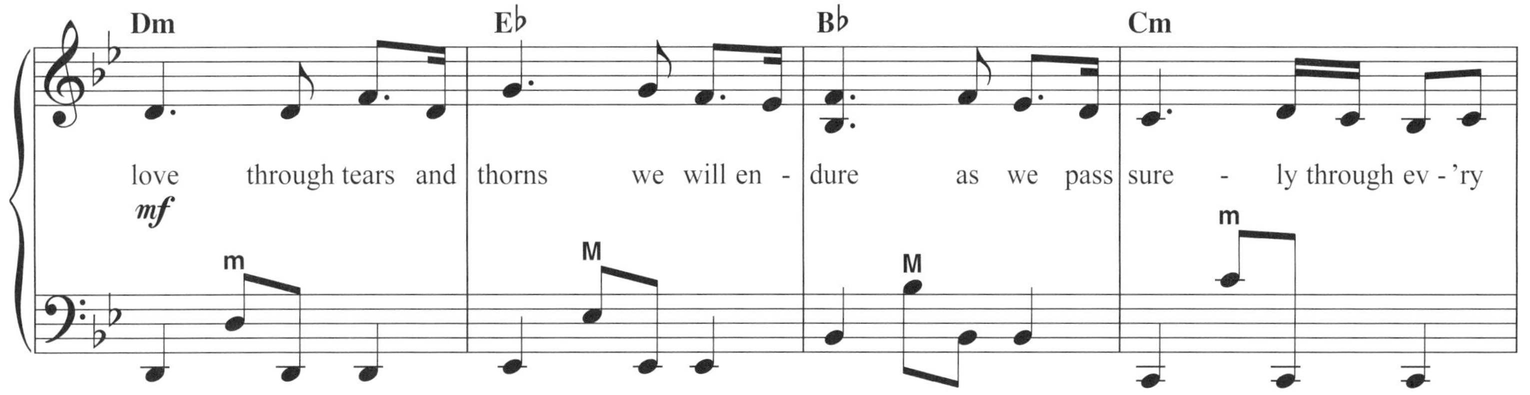
Dm
E♭
B♭
Cm
love through tears and thorns we will en - dure as we pass sure - ly through ev - 'ry
mf
m
M
M
m

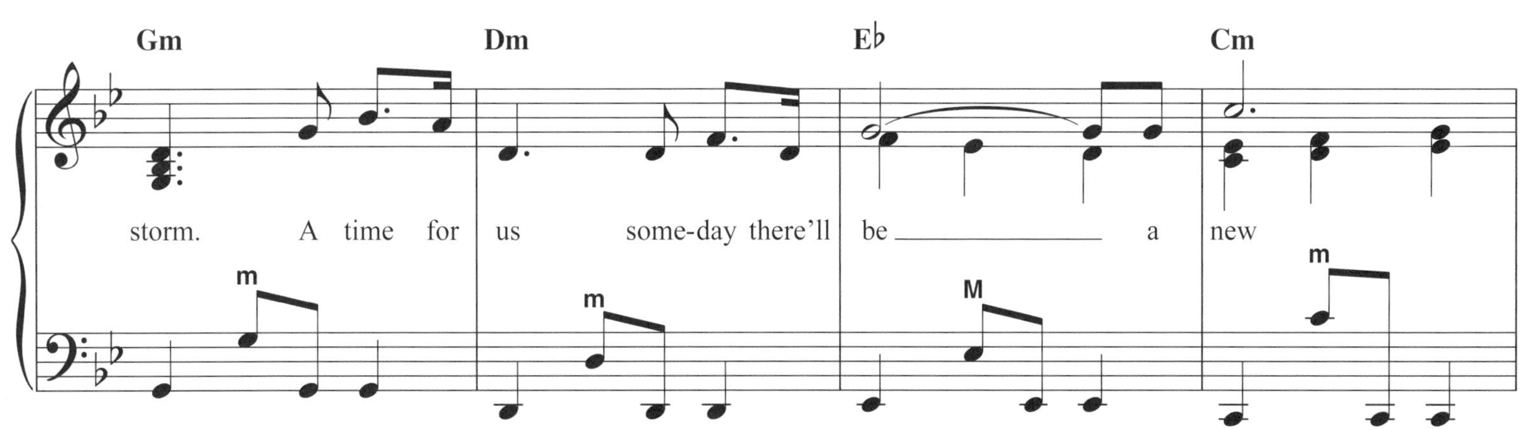
Gm
Dm
E♭
Cm
storm. A time for us some-day there'll be a new
m
m
M
m

Dm
Gm
Dm
Gm
world, a world of shin - ing hope for you, a world of shin - ing
mp
m
m
m
m

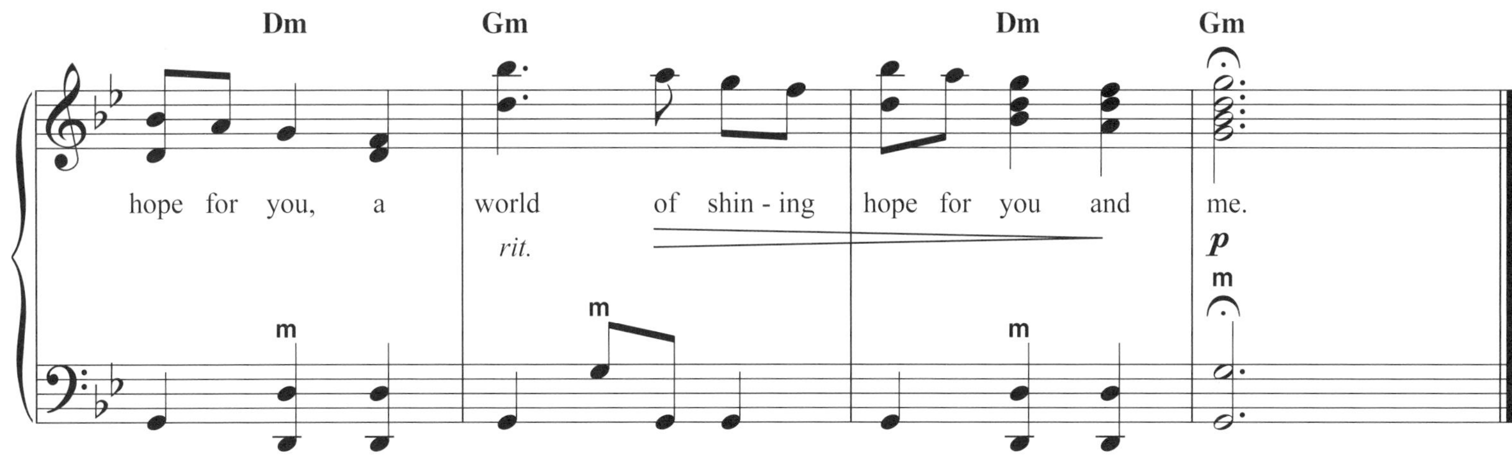
Dm
Gm
Dm
Gm
hope for you, a world of shin - ing hope for you and me.
rit.
p
m
m
m
m

WHEN SHE LOVED ME

from TOY STORY 2

Music and Lyrics by
RANDY NEWMAN

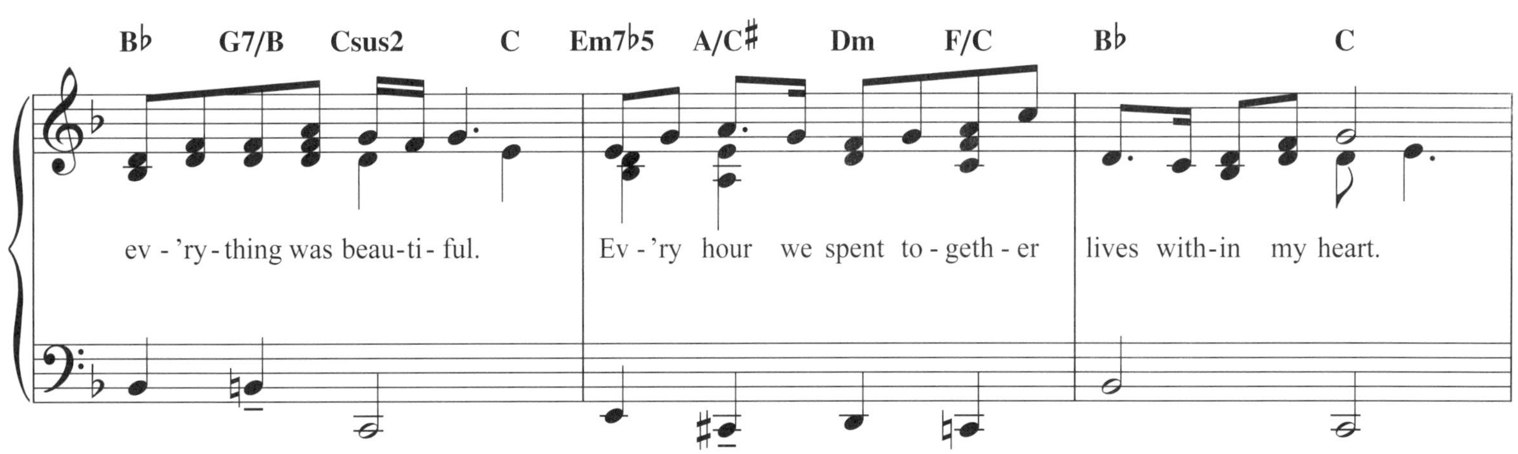

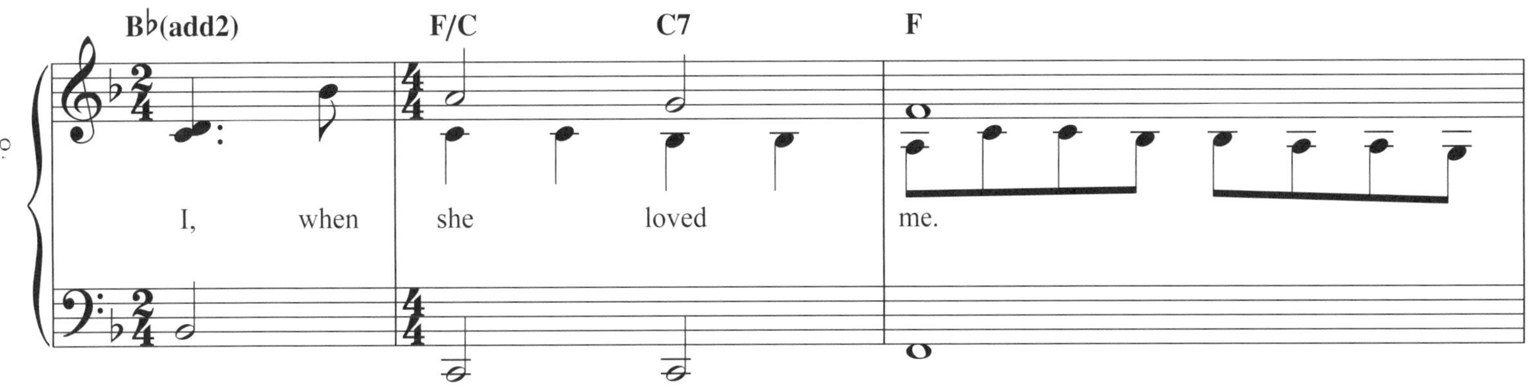
B♭(add2)
F/C
C7
F
I, when
she
loved
me.

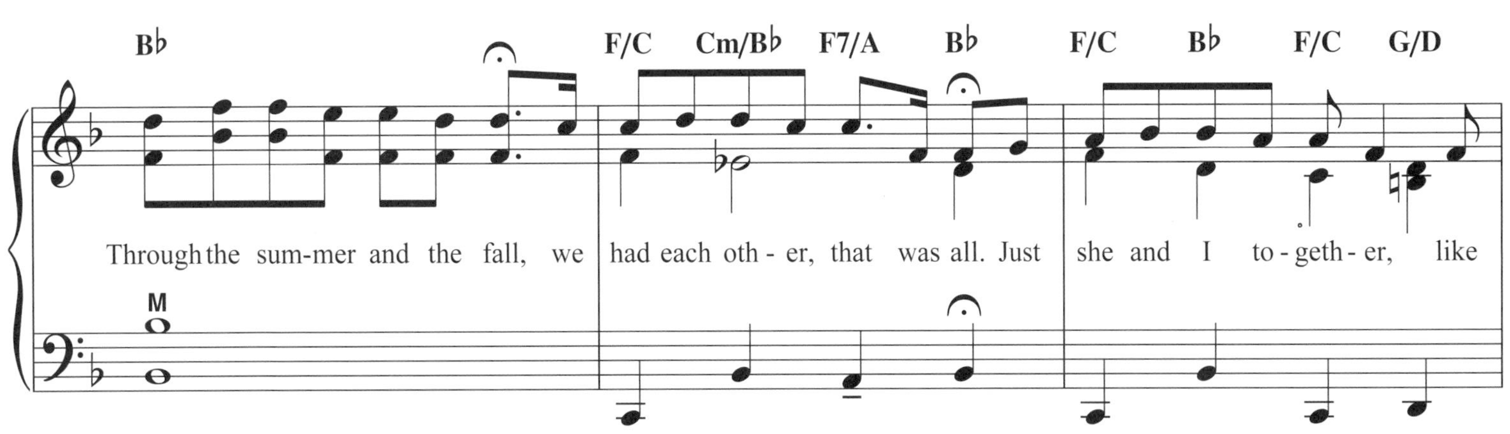
B♭
F/C
Cm/B♭
F7/A
B♭
F/C
B♭
F/C
G/D
Through the sum-mer and the fall, we
had each oth - er, that was all. Just
she and I to - geth - er, like
M

G7/B
C
F
Gm7
F/A
B♭
G7/B
Csus2
C
it was meant to be.
And when she was lone - ly,
I was there to com - fort her, and I

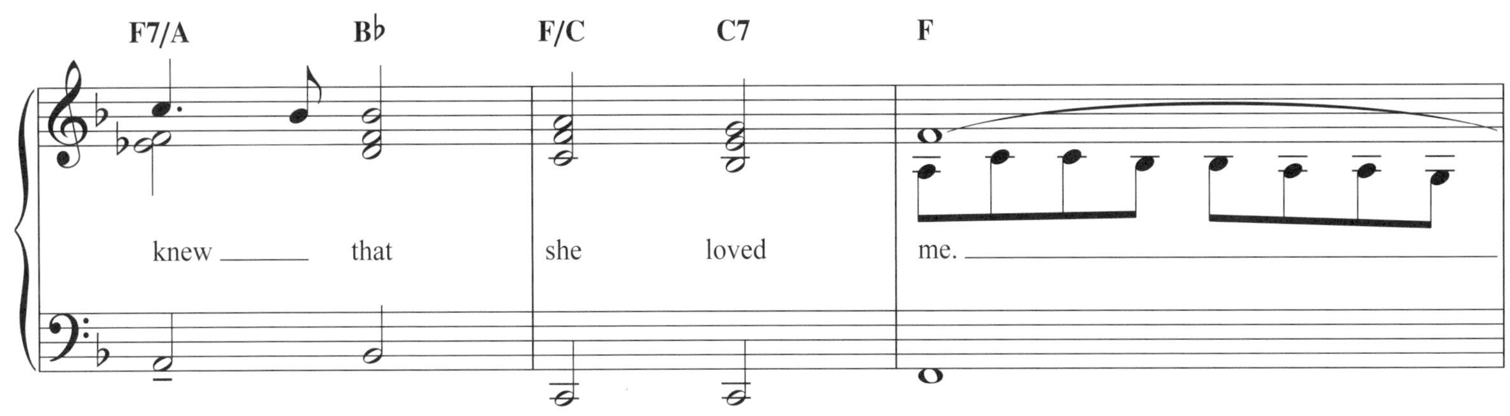
F7/A
B♭
F/C
C7
F
knew that
she loved
me.

Dm
B♭m6/D♭
F/C
So the years went by; I stayed the same. But

G/B
Gdim/B♭
F/A
Fm6/A♭
E♭/B♭
A7
Dm
B♭m6/D♭
C7
A♭m/C♭
B♭7
she be - gan to drift a - way; I was left a - lone. Still I wait - ed for the day

G♭6/D♭
A♭m/C
C7/E
when she'd say, "I will al - ways love you."

F
Gm7
F/A
B♭
G7/B
Csus2
C
Lone - ly and for - got - ten, nev - er thought she'd look my way, and she

Em7♭5 A/C♯ Dm F/C B♭ C F7/A B♭
smiled at me and held me just like she used to do, like she loved me when she

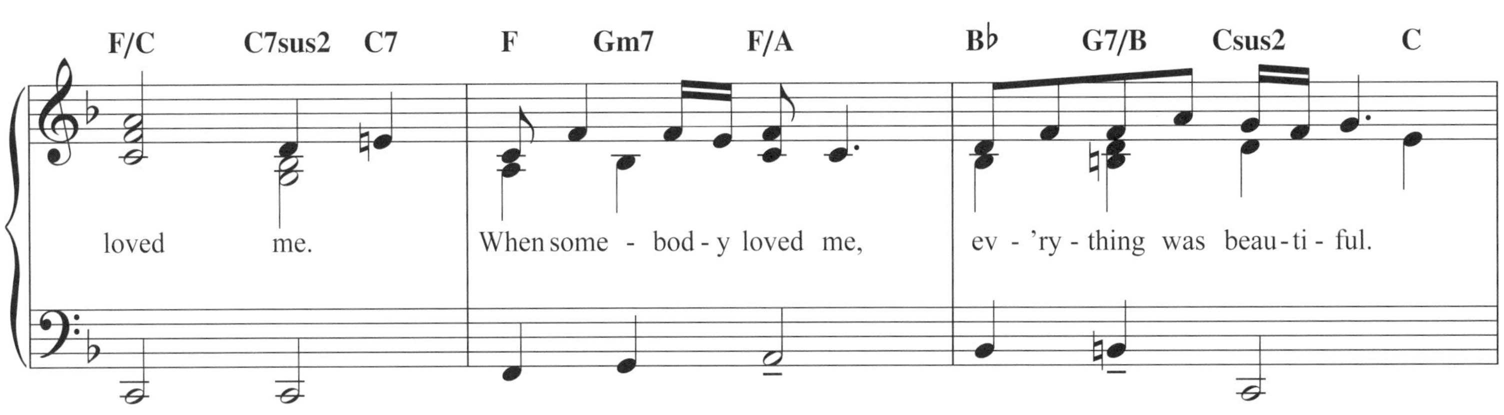
F/C C7sus2 C7 F Gm7 F/A B♭ G7/B Csus2 C
loved me. When some - bod - y loved me, ev - 'ry - thing was beau - ti - ful.

Em7♭5 A/C♯ Dm F/C B♭ C F/C C7
Ev - 'ry hour we spent to - geth - er lives with-in my heart, when she loved

F
me.

WHERE DO I BEGIN

(Love Theme)

from the Paramount Picture LOVE STORY

Words by CARL SIGMAN
Music by FRANCIS LAI

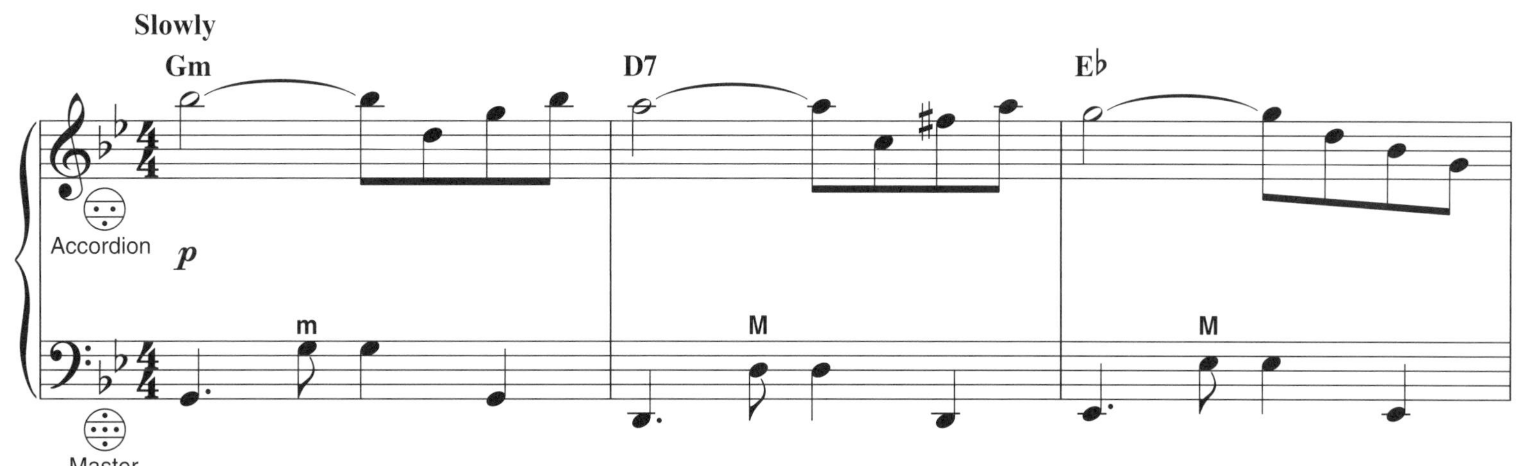

1.
E♭maj7
D7
the sim - ple truth a - bout the
she came in - to my life and
love she brings to me?
made the liv - ing fine.
Where do I
M
7

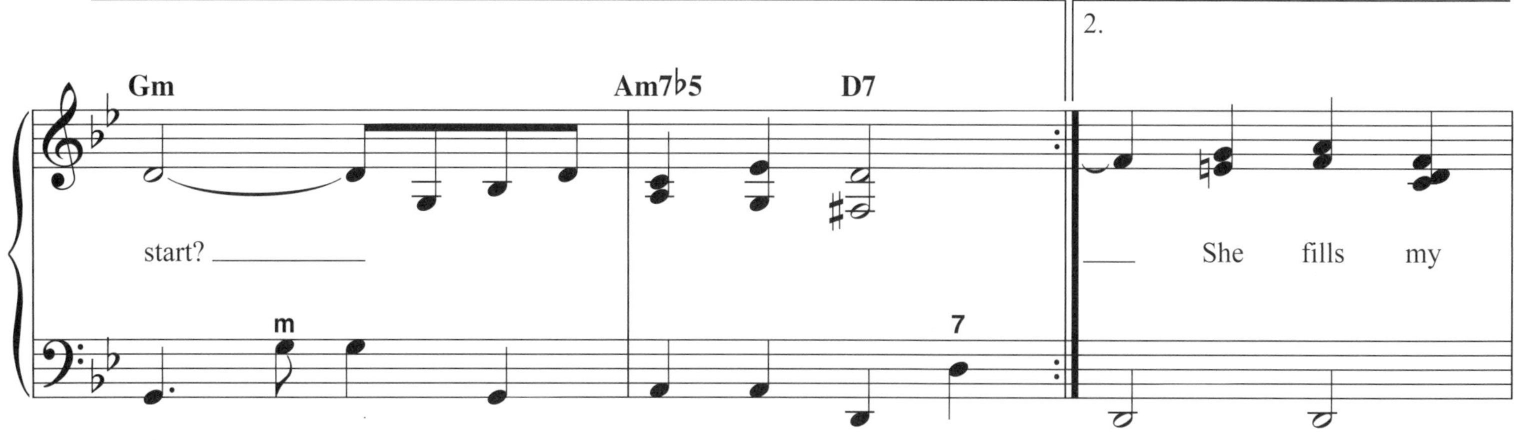
2.
Gm
Am7♭5
D7
start?
She fills my
m
7

Gmaj7
G7
Cm
heart.
She fills my
heart with ver - y
f
M
m

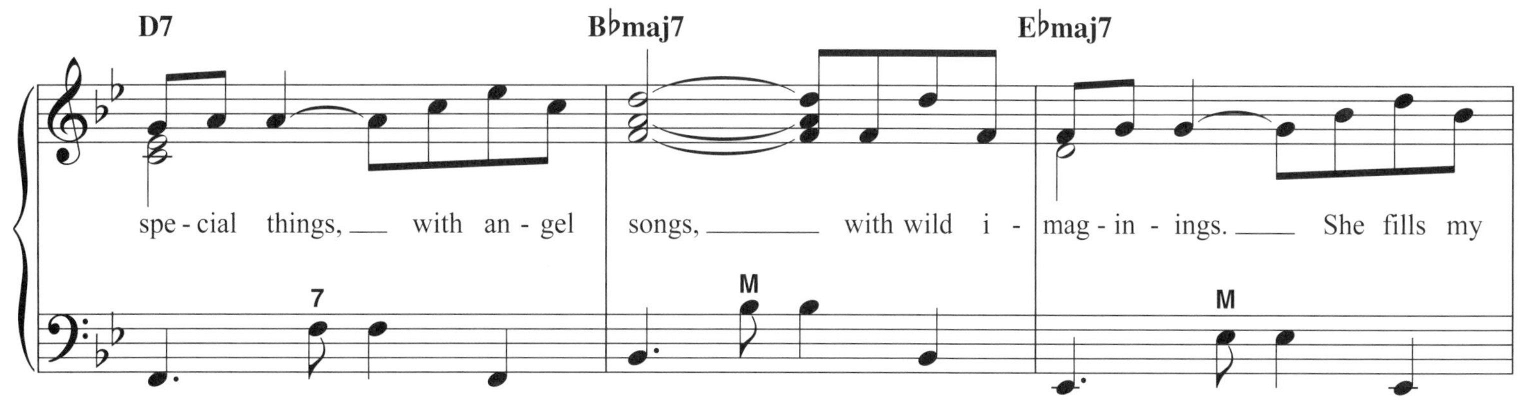
D7
B♭maj7
E♭maj7
spe - cial things, with an - gel
songs, with wild i -
mag - in - ings. She fills my
7
M
M

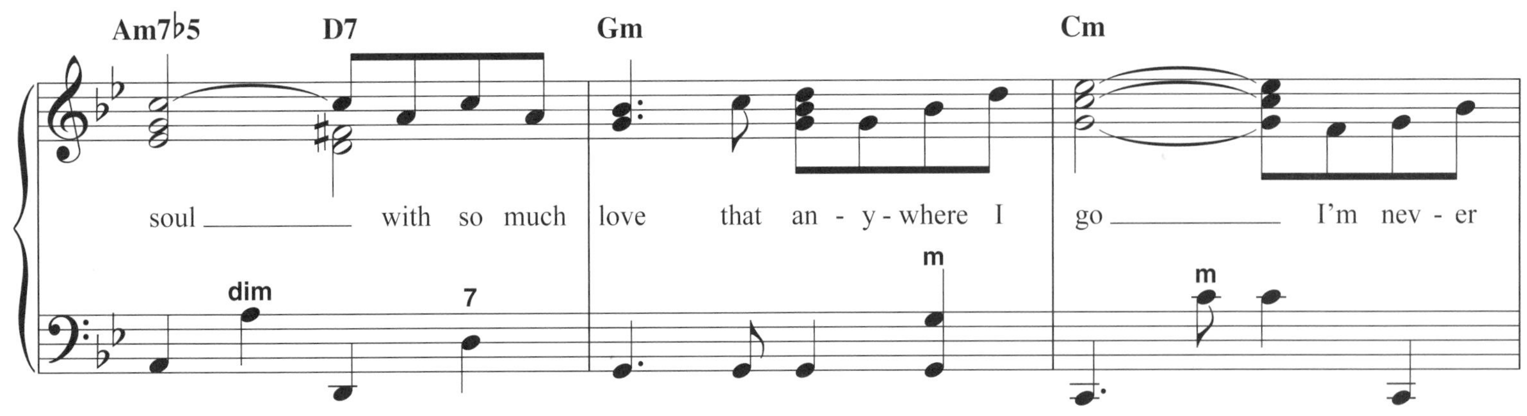
Am7♭5
D7
Gm
Cm
soul ___ with so much love that an - y - where I go ___ I'm nev - er
dim
7
m
m

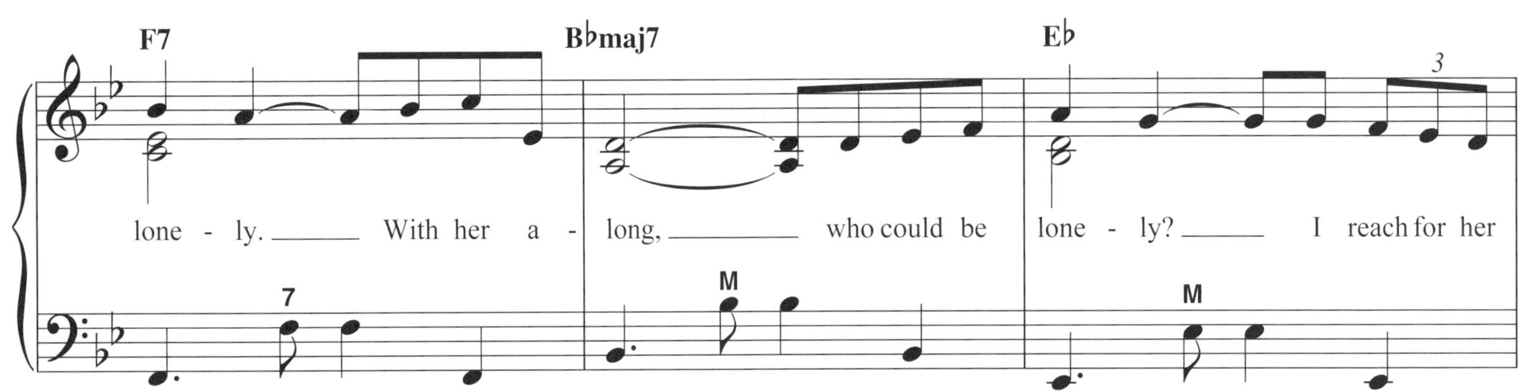
F7
B♭maj7
E♭
3
lone - ly. ___ With her a - long, ___ who could be lone - ly? ___ I reach for her
7
M
M

A7
Dmaj7
D7
hand; ___ it's al - ways there. ___
7

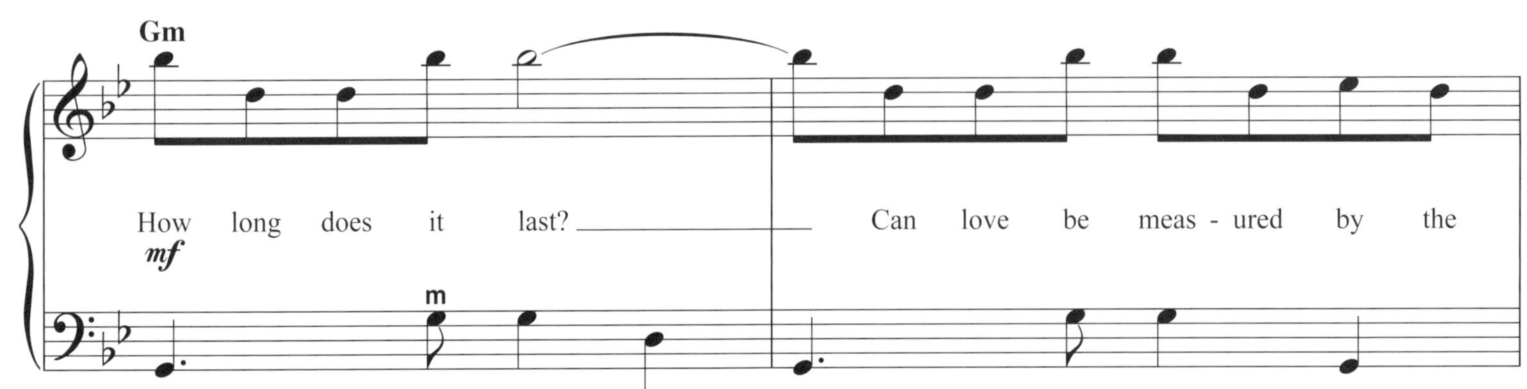
Gm
How long does it last? ___ Can love be meas - ured by the
mf
m

D7
Gm
ho - urs in a day?
I have no an - swers now, but
this much I can say:
7
m

E♭maj7
D7
I know I'll need her till the
stars all burn a - way,
and she'll be
M
7

Gm
D7
there.
m
7

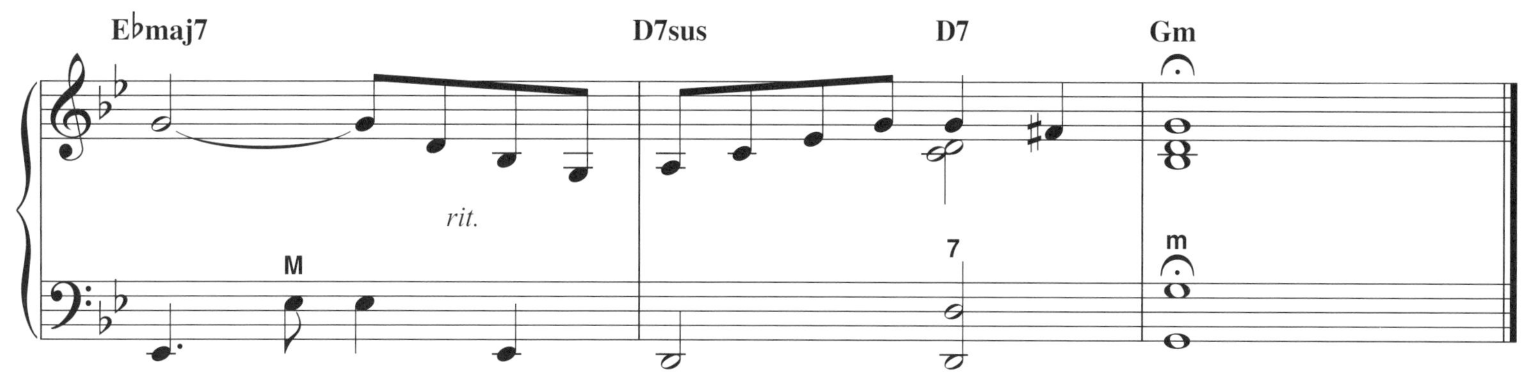
E♭maj7
D7sus
D7
Gm
rit.
M
7
m

THE WINDMILLS OF YOUR MIND

Theme from THE THOMAS CROWN AFFAIR

Words by ALAN and MARILYN BERGMAN
Music by MICHEL LEGRAND

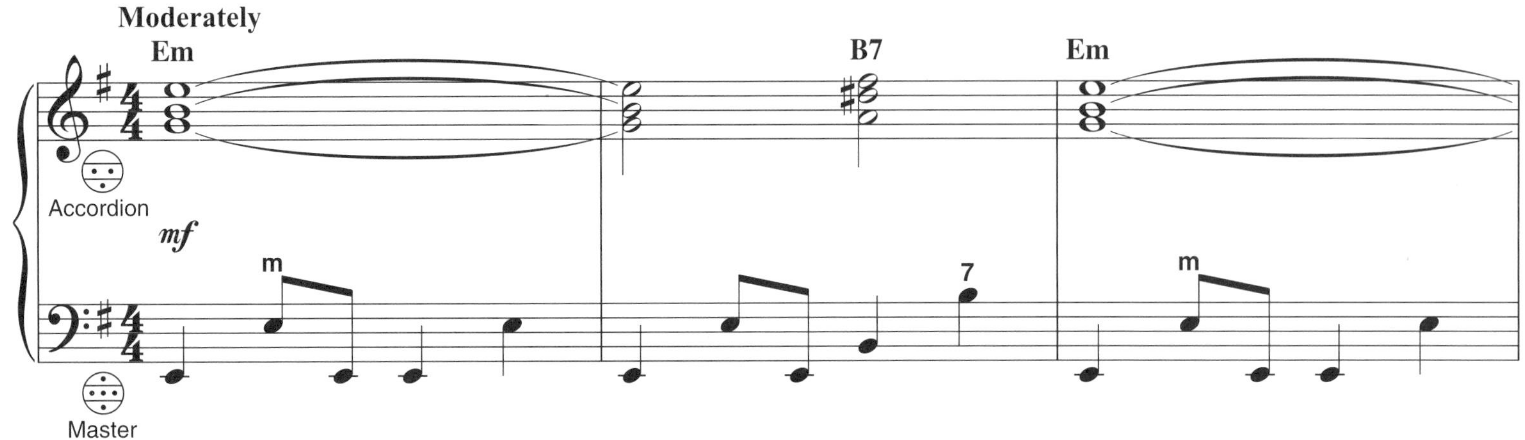

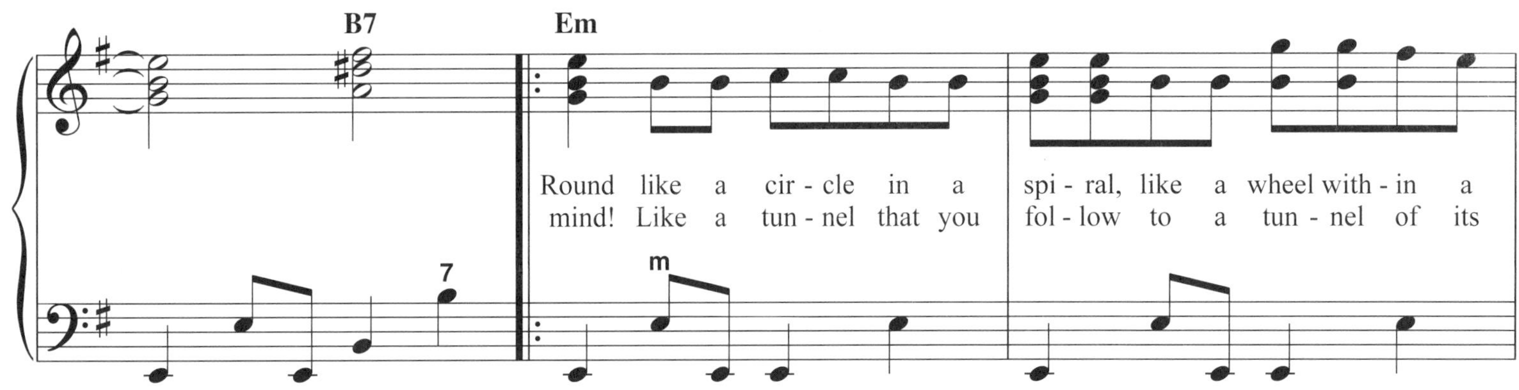

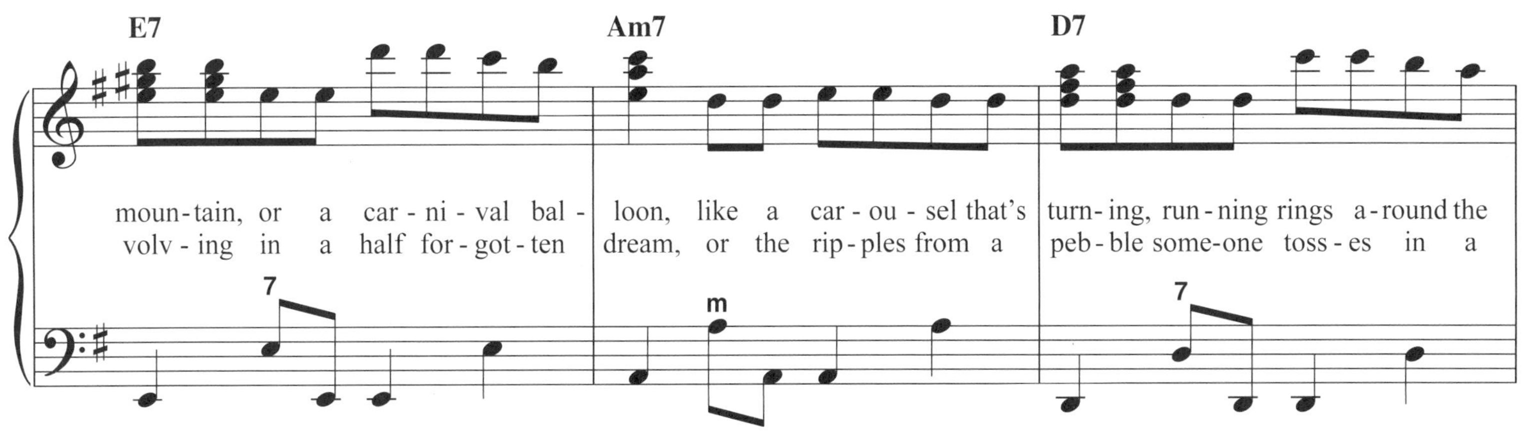
E7
Am7
D7
moun-tain, or a car-ni-val bal- loon, like a car-ou-sel that's turn-ing, run-ning rings a-round the
volv-ing in a half for-got-ten dream, or the rip-ples from a peb-ble some-one toss-es in a
7
m
7

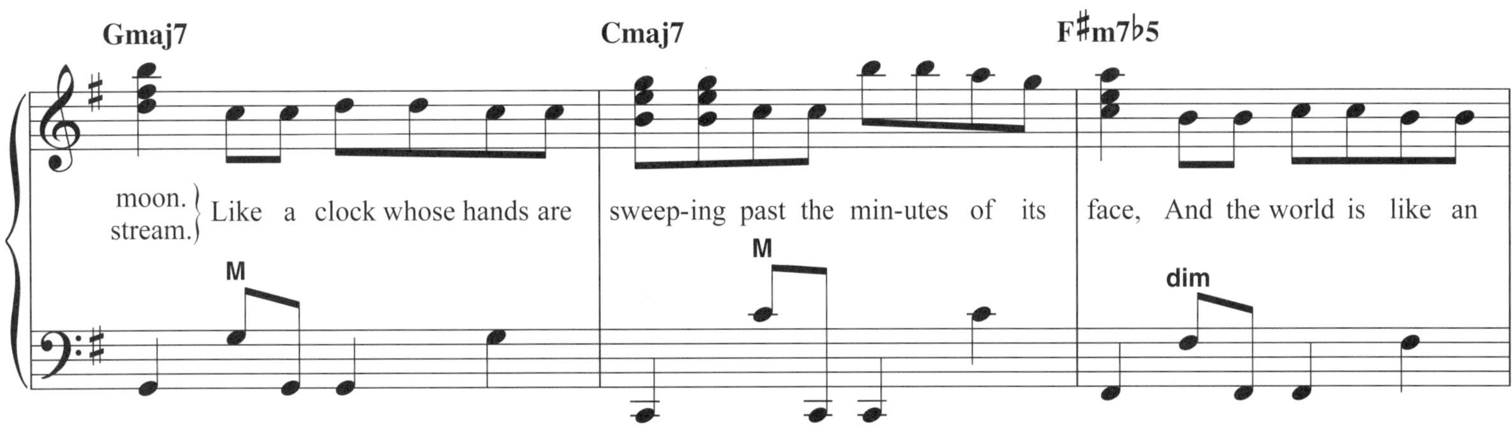
Gmaj7
Cmaj7
F♯m7♭5
moon.
stream.
Like a clock whose hands are sweep-ing past the min-utes of its face, And the world is like an
M
M
dim

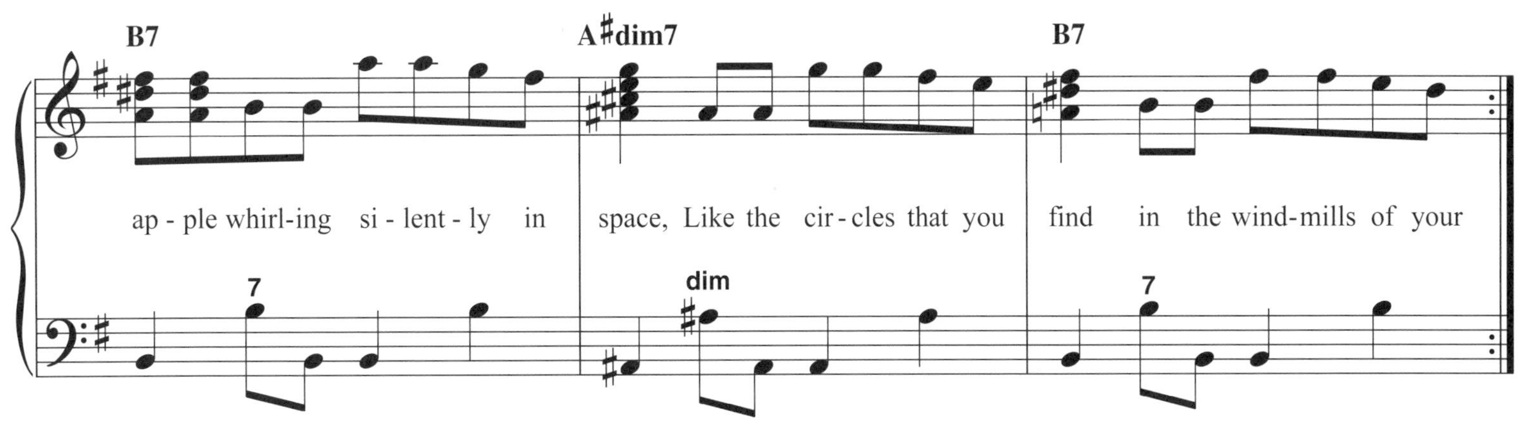
B7
A♯dim7
B7
ap-ple whirl-ing si-lent-ly in space, Like the cir-cles that you find in the wind-mills of your
7
dim
7

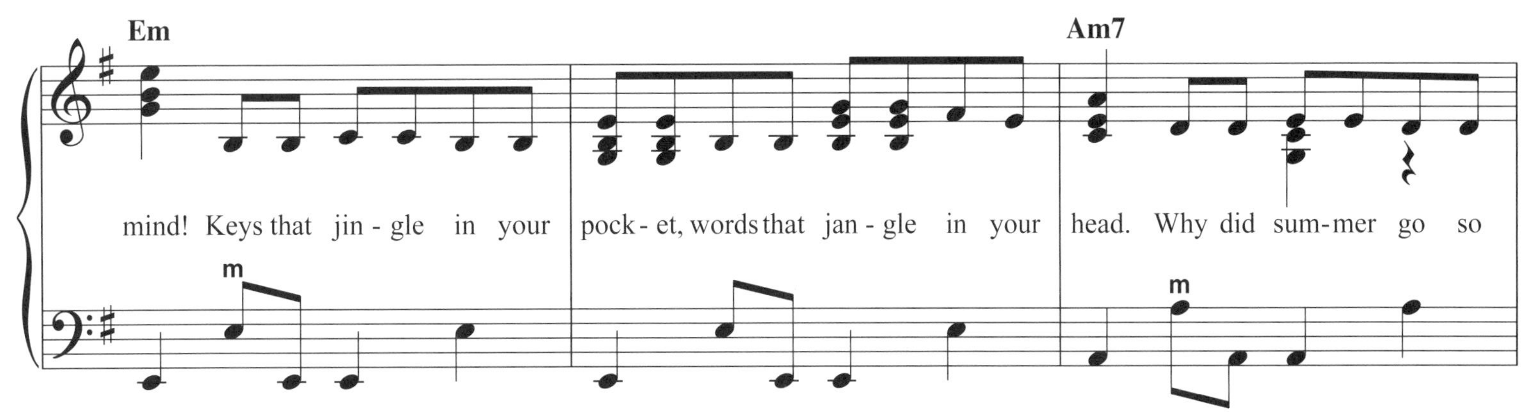
Em
Am7
mind! Keys that jin-gle in your pock-et, words that jan-gle in your head. Why did sum-mer go so
m
m

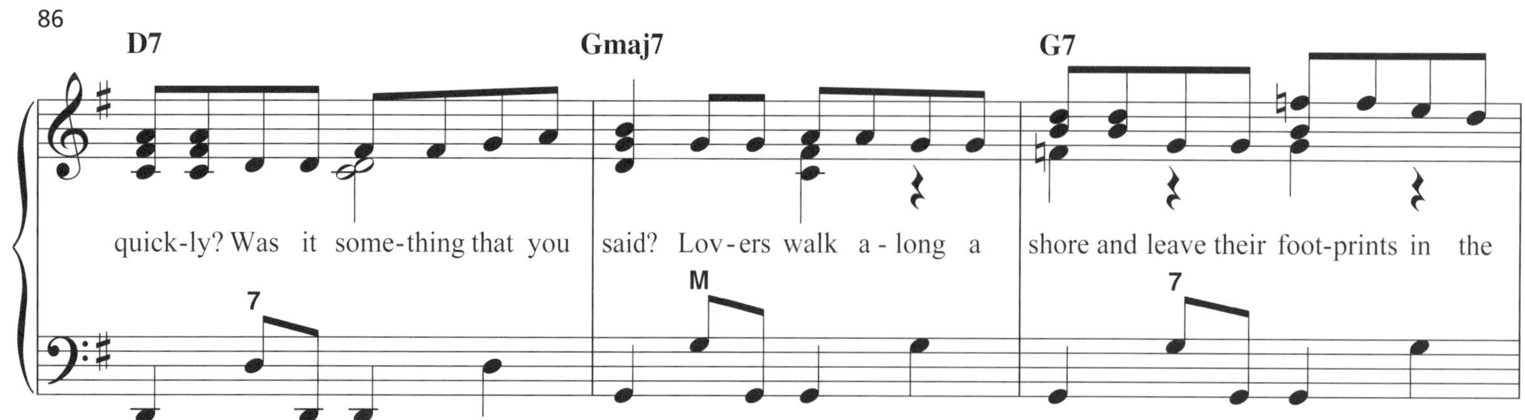
D7
Gmaj7
G7
quick-ly? Was it some-thing that you said? Lov-ers walk a-long a shore and leave their foot-prints in the
7
M
7

Cmaj7
F♯7
Bm
sand. Is the sound of dis-tant drum-ming just the fin-gers of your hand? Pic-tures hang-ing in a
M
7
m

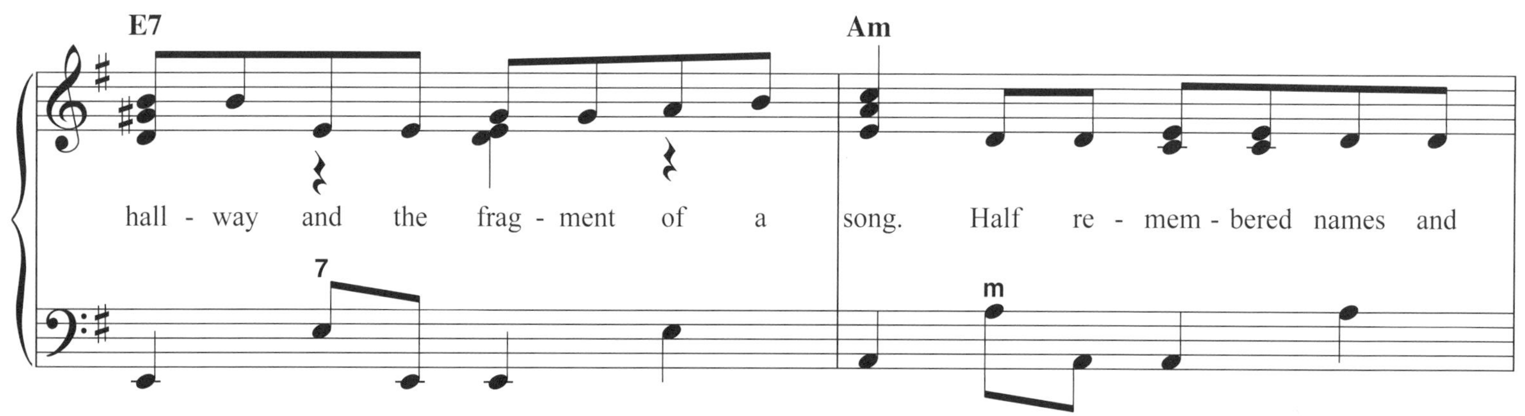
E7
Am
hall - way and the frag - ment of a song. Half re - mem - bered names and
7
m

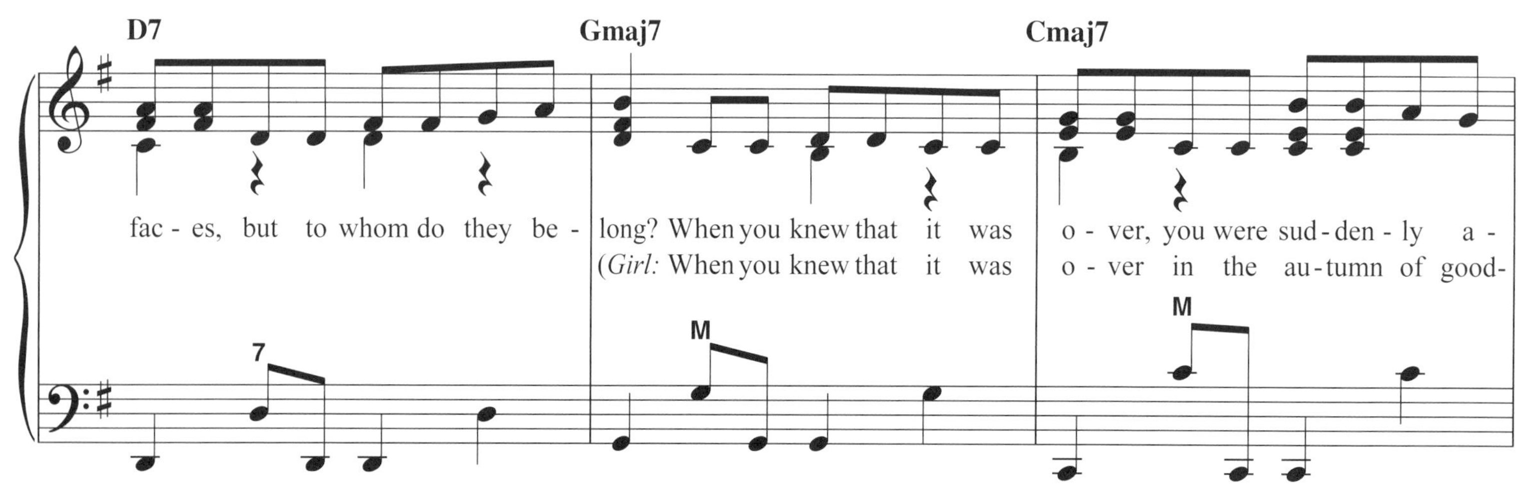
D7
Gmaj7
Cmaj7
fac - es, but to whom do they be - long? When you knew that it was o - ver, you were sud-den - ly a -
(Girl: When you knew that it was o - ver in the au-tumn of good-
7
M
M

F♯m7♭5
B7
ware That the au - tumn leaves were turn - ing to the col - or of her
byes, For a mo - ment you could not re - call the col - or of his
dim
7

Em
B7
hair! Like a cir - cle in a spi - ral, like a wheel with - in a wheel, Nev - er end - ing or be -
eyes!)
m
7

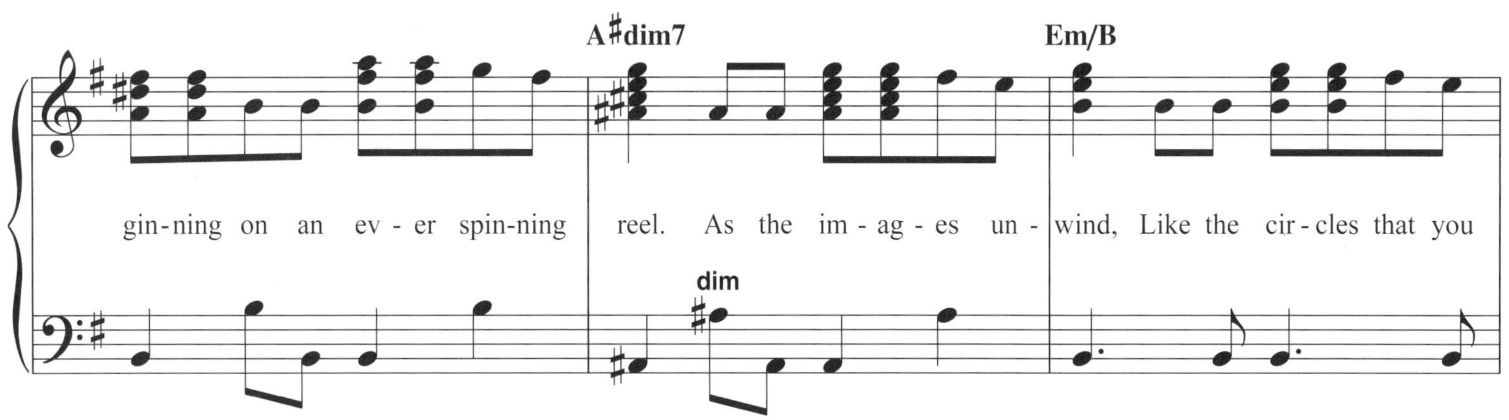
A♯dim7
Em/B
gin - ning on an ev - er spin - ning reel. As the im - ag - es un - wind, Like the cir - cles that you
dim

B7
Em
find in the wind - mills of your mind!
7
m

A COLLECTION OF ALL-TIME FAVORITES
FOR ACCORDION

ACCORDION FAVORITES
arr. Gary Meisner
16 all-time favorites, arranged for accordion, including: Can't Smile Without You • Could I Have This Dance • Endless Love • Memory • Sunrise, Sunset • I.O.U. • and more.
00359012..$12.99

ALL-TIME FAVORITES FOR ACCORDION
arr. Gary Meisner
20 must-know standards arranged for accordions. Includes: Ain't Misbehavin' • Autumn Leaves • Crazy • Hello, Dolly! • Hey, Good Lookin' • Moon River • Speak Softly, Love • Unchained Melody • The Way We Were • Zip-A-Dee-Doo-Dah • and more.
00311088..$10.95

THE BEATLES FOR ACCORDION
17 hits from the Lads from Liverpool have been arranged for accordion. Includes: All You Need Is Love • Eleanor Rigby • The Fool on the Hill • Here Comes the Sun • Hey Jude • In My Life • Let It Be • Ob-La-Di, Ob-La-Da • Penny Lane • When I'm Sixty-Four • Yesterday • and more.
00268724 ....$14.99

BROADWAY FAVORITES
arr. Ken Kotwitz
A collection of 17 wonderful show songs, including: Don't Cry for Me Argentina • Getting to Know You • If I Were a Rich Man • Oklahoma • People Will Say We're in Love • We Kiss in a Shadow.
00490157..$10.99

DISNEY SONGS FOR ACCORDION – 3RD EDITION
13 Disney favorites especially arranged for accordion, including: Be Our Guest • Beauty and the Beast • Can You Feel the Love Tonight • Chim Chim Cher-ee • It's a Small World • Let It Go • Under the Sea • A Whole New World • You'll Be in My Heart • Zip-A-Dee-Doo-Dah • and more!
00152508 ....$12.99

FIRST 50 SONGS YOU SHOULD PLAY ON THE ACCORDION
arr. Gary Meisner
If you're new to the accordion, you are probably eager to learn some songs. This book provides 50 simplified arrangements of must-know popular standards, folk songs and show tunes, including: All of Me • Beer Barrel Polka • Carnival of Venice • Edelweiss • Hava Nagila (Let's Be Happy) • Hernando's Hideaway • Jambalaya (On the Bayou) • Lady of Spain • Moon River • 'O Sole Mio • Sentimental Journey • Somewhere, My Love • That's Amore (That's Love) • Under Paris Skies • and more. Includes lyrics when applicable.
00250269 ....$14.99

FRENCH SONGS FOR ACCORDION
arr. Gary Meisner
A très magnifique collection of 17 French standards arranged for the accordion. Includes: Autumn Leaves • Beyond the Sea • C'est Magnifique • I Love Paris • La Marseillaise • Let It Be Me (Je T'appartiens) • Under Paris Skies • Watch What Happens • and more.
00311498..$9.99

HYMNS FOR ACCORDION
arr. Gary Meisner
24 treasured sacred favorites arranged for accordion, including: Amazing Grace • Beautiful Savior • Come, Thou Fount of Every Blessing • Crown Him with Many Crowns • Holy, Holy, Holy • It Is Well with My Soul • Just a Closer Walk with Thee • A Mighty Fortress Is Our God • Nearer, My God, to Thee • The Old Rugged Cross • Rock of Ages • What a Friend We Have in Jesus • and more.
00277160 ....$9.99

ITALIAN SONGS FOR ACCORDION
arr. Gary Meisner
17 favorite Italian standards arranged for accordion, including: Carnival of Venice • Ciribiribin • Come Back to Sorrento • Funiculi, Funicula • La donna è mobile • La Spagnola • 'O Sole Mio • Santa Lucia • Tarantella • and more.
00311089..$9.95

LATIN FAVORITES FOR ACCORDION
arr. Gary Meisner
20 Latin favorites, including: Bésame Mucho (Kiss Me Much) • The Girl from Ipanema • How Insensitive (Insensatez) • Perfidia • Spanish Eyes • So Nice (Summer Samba) • and more.
00310932..$12.99

THE FRANK MAROCCO ACCORDION SONGBOOK
This songbook includes arrangements and recordings of 15 standards and original songs from legendary jazz accordionist Frank Marocco, including: All the Things You Are • Autumn Leaves • Beyond the Sea • Moon River • Moonlight in Vermont • Stormy Weather (Keeps Rainin' All the Time) • and more!
00233441 Book/Online Audio..............$19.99

POP STANDARDS FOR ACCORDION
Arrangements of 20 Classic Songs
20 classic pop standards arranged for accordion are included in this collection: Annie's Song • Chances Are • For Once in My Life • Help Me Make It Through the Night • My Cherie Amour • Ramblin' Rose • (Sittin' On) The Dock of the Bay • That's Amore (That's Love) • Unchained Melody • and more.
00254822 ....$12.99

POLKA FAVORITES
arr. Kenny Kotwitz
An exciting new collection of 16 songs, including: Beer Barrel Polka • Liechtensteiner Polka • My Melody of Love • Paloma Blanca • Pennsylvania Polka • Too Fat Polka • and more.
00311573..$10.95

STAR WARS FOR ACCORDION
A dozen songs from the Star Wars franchise: The Imperial March (Darth Vader's Theme) • Luke and Leia • March of the Resistance • Princess Leia's Theme • Rey's Theme • Star Wars (Main Theme) • and more.
00157380 ....$12.99

TANGOS FOR ACCORDION
arr. Gary Meisner
Every accordionist needs to know some tangos! Here are 15 favorites: Amapola (Pretty Little Poppy) • Aquellos Ojos Verdes (Green Eyes) • Hernando's Hideaway • Jalousie (Jealousy) • Kiss of Fire • La Cumparsita (The Masked One) • Quizás, Quizás, Quizás (Perhaps, Perhaps, Perhaps) • The Rain in Spain • Tango of Roses • Whatever Lola Wants (Lola Gets) • and more!
00122252 ....$9.99

3-CHORD SONGS FOR ACCORDION
arr. Gary Meisner
Here are nearly 30 songs that are easy to play but still sound great! Includes: Amazing Grace • Can Can • Danny Boy • For He's a Jolly Good Fellow • He's Got the Whole World in His Hands • Just a Closer Walk with Thee • La Paloma Blanca (The White Dove) • My Country, 'Tis of Thee • Ode to Joy • Oh! Susanna • Yankee Doodle • The Yellow Rose of Texas • and more.
00312104 ....$9.99

LAWRENCE WELK'S POLKA FOLIO
More than 50 famous polkas, schottisches and waltzes arranged for piano and accordion, including: Blue Eyes • Budweiser Polka • Clarinet Polka • Cuckoo Polka • The Dove Polka • Draw One Polka • Gypsy Polka • Helena Polka • International Waltzes • Let's Have Another One • Schnitzelbank • Shuffle Schottische • Squeeze Box Polka • Waldteuful Waltzes • and more.
00123218..$12.99

HAL•LEONARD®
Visit Hal Leonard Online at
www.halleonard.com

1119
129